HOPE OF *Glory*

Advance Praise for Hope of Glory

"There are many things in the realm of the Christian Church which may be regarded as "add-on" and "optional extra." However, it should be emphasized that theology and mission must never fall into those categories. These must always be at the beating heart of Church life. This book is the product of knowing God and serving God. May it also fulfill our Savior's prayer in the lives of each reader 'that they know you, the only true God, and Jesus Christ, whom you have sent' (John 17:3)."

—Geoff Fox, Elder
Haven Church, Gorran Haven, Cornwall

"This book explains vitally important spiritual truths like judgment and salvation and illustrates these truths by showing how God has worked in the lives of people of faith. The book makes it clear that all of us will one day meet our Maker and that now is the time to seek God's kingdom. Jason's experience as a missionary makes him ideally qualified to write this book. I hope that every reader will discover hope in salvation and God's glory."

—Professor Stuart Burgess, BSc, PhD, CEng, FIMechE
Author of over two hundred scientific papers
on design in engineering and nature
and author/co-author of over ten books on Creation

"Jason Murfitt is a man on a mission, and this book reveals his passion. His life is committed to telling people about Jesus Christ so that they can know Him as their Savior and Lord. He also wants to encourage

Christians in their faith so that they realize all the blessings that are theirs in Jesus and serve Him in the work of His Kingdom. The great theme of this book is God Himself and the way He graciously meets us in the midst of our daily lives, which are often complicated and troubled. He introduces us to a wide range of people who have all experienced God's grace and love in Jesus and who are looking forward to being with Jesus in Heaven."

—Peter Milsom
Former Chairman for the British Evangelical Council, Director of Affinity, and Director of UFM Worldwide and current Associate Consultant for UFM

"Here is a book to encourage and challenge. Jason writes with clarity and warmth, pointing us to our Savior. Accounts of the famous, historical, and ordinary speak of the power of the gospel in salvation. I warmly recommend *Hope of Glory*."

—Daryl Jones
Mission Director of Grace Baptist Mission

"In this evangelistic book, Jason presents a concise and accessible defense of the Christian faith, ideal for those who are skeptical or just curious to learn more. Jason winsomely challenges the reader with key tenets of biblical teaching about the character of God, the gospel, and practical Christian living. He skillfully weaves together words of testimony from a range of sources as he makes his case—from St. Augustine to Little Richard—and vividly draws upon his own experiences as a missionary in the Brazilian rainforest. Warmly recommended."

—John Tredgett, Elder
Grace Evangelical Church, Carlisle

"Is Christianity true? What is God like? How can I find peace with God? Where will I spend eternity? Jason Murfitt answers these questions in a wonderfully engaging fashion, drawing on the lives, writings, and experiences of a wide variety of witnesses. He introduces us to those who speak to these questions—from a great theologian to a contemporary musician, from a fisherman in the Brazilian rainforest to a tree surgeon in the UK, and Christians from the early church, the seventeenth century, and the modern day. There is much here to help those who are exploring the Christian faith and rich resources for those who are already Christians who want to grow in understanding."

—*Bill James, Principal*
London Seminary

HOPE OF Glory

**Ten Lives Transformed by a
Close Encounter of the Heavenly Kind**

JASON MURFITT

Ambassador International
GREENVILLE, SOUTH CAROLINA & BELFAST, NORTHERN IRELAND

www.ambassador-international.com

Hope of Glory
Ten Lives Transformed by a Close Encounter of the Heavenly Kind
©2025 by Jason Murfitt
All rights reserved

ISBN: 978-1-64960-888-8 , hard cover
ISBN: 978-1-64960-428-6, paperback
eISBN: 978-1-64960-476-7

Cover Design by Karen Slayne
Interior Typesetting by Dentelle Design
Edited by Katie Cruice Smith
Original portraits drawn by Tea Furus

No part of this publication may be reproduced, distributed, or transmitted in any form or by any means, including photocopying, recording, or other electronic or mechanical methods, without the prior written permission of the publisher, except in the case of brief quotations embodied in critical reviews and certain other noncommercial uses permitted by copyright law. For permission requests, contact the publisher using the information below.

Scripture marked KJV taken from the King James Version of the Bible. Public domain.

Scriptures marked NIV taken from the Holy Bible, New International Version®, NIV® Copyright ©1973, 1978, 1984, 2011 by Biblica, Inc.® Used by permission. All rights reserved worldwide.

Ambassador International titles may be purchased in bulk for education, business, fundraising, or sales promotional use. For information, please email sales@emeraldhouse.com.

AMBASSADOR INTERNATIONAL
Emerald House
411 University Ridge, Suite B14
Greenville, SC 29601
United States
www.ambassador-international.com

AMBASSADOR BOOKS
The Mount
2 Woodstock Link
Belfast, BT6 8DD
Northern Ireland, United Kingdom
www.ambassadormedia.co.uk

The colophon is a trademark of Ambassador, a Christian publishing company.

"I believe so that I may understand."

—Anselm of Canterbury

Table of Contents

Foreword   1

Preface   3

CHAPTER 1
The God Who Speaks   5

CHAPTER 2
The God Who Is   17

CHAPTER 3
The God Who Judges   39

CHAPTER 4
The God to Be Feared   49

CHAPTER 5
The God Who Pursues   59

CHAPTER 6
The God Who Is Merciful   69

CHAPTER 7
The God We Serve 85

CHAPTER 8
The God Who Saves for His Glory 103

CHAPTER 9
The God Who Gives Hope 123

APPENDIX A
The Origin of Evil Explored 133

APPENDIX B
What Is Eternity? 141

Additional Resources 143
Bibliography 145
About the Author 149

Foreword

I remember a time in my childhood when I was hungry all the time, and—joy of joys!—a rich businessman from the Far East invited our whole family out for a meal. There were twelve courses, followed by coffee and chocolates, and the event lasted a whole evening. I have often wondered how long it took for that feast to be prepared.

What an array of foods was paraded before us! I didn't know what some of them were, and our host had to explain. I also noticed that while some of the dishes just slipped down, there were others which required quite a lot of cutting and chewing. They were equally delicious and nutritious, but we all had to slow down to get through them. I went to bed well-fed, happy, and with only one slight disappointment—there were no bread and jam!

In this book, Jason Murfitt invites us to a similar meal—not for the body, but for the mind and soul. Who knows how long it has taken him to prepare it? There are nine courses, and those who are the hungriest will enjoy them best and get the greatest benefit. What a variety of flavors and textures is waiting for every reader! But don't be surprised to find that some of the dishes just slip down, while others require a slower approach and a bit more chewing.

If there are items on the menu which are unfamiliar to you, please don't worry. Your good host will explain everything to you.

And if you don't find your favorite bread and jam, throw away your disappointment. Savor and digest what has been prepared for you, revel in the experience of being well-fed, go through life with God, and die to enjoy Him forever.

—*Stuart Olyott*
Pastor and author of numerous Christian books

Preface

It was January 2020. I had driven until nothing was familiar and ventured into an ancient woodland to draw close to God for a day of prayer. The cold and drizzle were predictable, but what happened next wasn't.

Within minutes, the book you are about to read flooded my mind almost in its entirety. There has, however, been one major development since then, and that's where you come in.

Originally, I thought my idea would develop into an evangelistic booklet that would present the basics of the Christian faith to the antagonist, skeptic, and atheist philosopher. But even in the woods that day, as I began to list their common objections against Christianity, to which I intended to respond, I could see in my mind's eye that the booklet's length and depth would be hard to rein in. It became a book!

Although saved at a young age, I made little progress in my Christian maturity for a number of years. This was because I had one foot in the church and the other lodged in the world. Then I got serious. As I rededicated my life to Christ, my hunger for truth became insatiable.

From that desire comes the evolution of this book, along with a prayer that it will be a useful apologetic tool for those who, like me, were formerly complacent and negligent toward the things of God but now possess a growing appetite for spiritual food, wanting to be more active in sharing their faith.

There was another list I made that day, a list of heroes of the faith whose contrasting lives illustrate the all-embracing power of God as His Word takes root. That's why I've given ample space to allow these imperfect trophies of grace to speak about God's dealings with them. They represent different continents, cultures, even centuries, but listen to their united chorus of love for Jesus, Who is Lord over all.

May *Hope of Glory* encourage you also to stand confidently on the same biblical ground as you give a reasonable defense to the antagonist, skeptic, and atheist philosopher, blessed to "contend for the faith that was once for all entrusted to God's holy people" (Jude 3).

CHAPTER 1
The God Who Speaks

"Help! I'm stuck!" This is what I *want* to scream, but pride prevents all but a whimper to escape from my trembling lips. Sweat trickles down my brow and stings my eyes. I'm too scared to wipe it away. I can't, anyway; I'm clinging to a tree for dear life. My harness is chafing me at every point of contact, and my legs are starting to spasm. Two iron spikes dig into my shins and pin me to the tree. I can't go up, and I can't go down.

What life choices did I make that brought me to this place and time? I had been ascending this large Monterey pine with nothing but a stiff rope looped around the tree and attached to my harness. And now the hoop is caught under the thick bark, and I am officially stuck. Fifty feet beneath me is the hard, unforgiving ground, where my new boss, Tommy, is staring up at me. I was trying to impress him on my first day at work.

He *had* asked, "Can you climb trees?"

To which I replied, "Sure."

"Have you much experience as a tree surgeon?"

"Some."

I hadn't lied; I had just never before climbed trees with spikes and a hooped rope. This terrifying situation I now find myself in is all new to me. And I'm scared of heights. Yes, a tree surgeon scared of heights. Crazy, but true.

On a wing and a prayer, I somehow manage to unstick myself, climb up another hundred feet into the crown of this giant tree, sit there for as long as possible to catch my breath, and recover my nerve before attempting to cut and lower down branches.

An hour later, I slump into the passenger seat of a battered Land Rover with a sandwich in one hand and a coffee in the other. The windows quickly steam up, especially as a hot conversation begins.

Tommy is seasoned in just about everything. Built like a bear—once with rippling muscles that are now padded and well-insulated—he looks weathered and burdened by life, irritated by the onset of old age. I try not to notice his broken trouser zipper, which yawns widely, or the twigs and leaves that seem to grow from him. After many years in the forest, it is hard to separate the man from the trees. He speaks softly with a droll tone that some might interpret as antagonism, but I hear one who is hungry for truth.

When I tell Tommy of my plans to be a missionary in Brazil, to teach people the Bible, he twitches a smile, unconvinced—perhaps because I am not yet thirty years old. He clears the condensation from the window and chuckles dryly. "Why do you think people there need your Bible?"

I take in a larger gulp of coffee than I intend, swallow hard, and respond, "Because it's God's Word. By it, we can know Who He is, what He's done, and how we should respond to Him."

Tommy cuts in, "But how can you know you can trust that the Bible *really* is God's Word? Who's to say that people haven't changed what God originally said? Or that God hasn't spoken at all?"

Although taken aback, I am thrilled, as it seems that Tommy is genuinely interested in knowing the answers to his questions. With more confidence now, I continue. "'In the beginning God . . .'[1] This is how our Creator begins His autobiography. Now, you either take God at His Word, or you don't. That *don't* category is larger than most realize. It includes everyone who says something like, 'I believe the Bible to a point'—the point being until it appears to conflict with science, or ever-changing social standards, or just personal preferences. The *don't* category also includes those who say something along the lines of 'I believe the Bible so far as it has been accurately preserved.'"

Tommy is very quick to interject. "What about all those translations? Don't they disagree in places? What ever happened to the original writings?"

I appreciate his objections and respond, "The original manuscripts—which, for example, the prophet Moses, or King David, or the apostle Peter wrote—have not survived. I think this was quite deliberately on God's part. He knows that we would have turned them into idols sooner or later. But they were copied, from which we now have many translations—some good, some not so good. These are translated from the thousands of ancient manuscripts and fragments that were copied throughout the centuries, which admittedly have not all been copied with the same degree of accuracy. But does that mean the Bible we have today is not what was preserved by God—that which He originally inspired?"[2]

Tommy smiles through his heavy stubble. It is impossible to know if he agrees or not, but he does seem interested, so I continue.

---

1 Genesis 1:1
2 2 Timothy 3:16-17

"Around twenty-five thousand New Testament and five thousand Old Testament manuscripts have been discovered to date. The Old Testament narrative spans from Creation, approximately sixty-four hundred years ago, until four hundred years B.C (before Jesus Christ was born). It was written between 1500 B.C to 400 B.C.

"The New Testament specifically covers a period of less than one hundred years, although the last book, Revelation, also projects forward to the end of days. The New Testament was written in the first century A.D between the 50s to 90s. No other collection of manuscripts from antiquity (that is, from before the sixteenth century) covering any other subject can compare. The closest contender for quantity of manuscripts is Homer's *Iliad*, which boasts a little over six hundred copies."

I notice his thoughtful silence as he takes a large bite of his sandwich. I don't want to complicate things but venture to say, "In fact, it is better that we have thousands of manuscripts for experts in the biblical languages to examine, as opposed to just one *untampered* original copy of the complete Bible locked away in a glass case in the back of a museum somewhere. Or worse, for it to become a type of holy grail on display for visitors to come and pay homage to. Who would look after it? Who would be allowed to see it? How would we know that it had not been tampered with? There would be nothing to compare it to.

"I have heard it said that we have eleven hundred pieces of a one-thousand-piece jigsaw. Nothing inspired by God has been lost, although some scribal errors and marginal notes have found their way into copies. But by comparing different lines of transmission and studying the consistency between copies that may well have been separated by centuries and copied in different continents, the errors and additions can be identified. This process gives credibility to the reliability of the Bible as God's Word."

I top up my coffee from the thermos and take a sip. It looks as if Tommy is weighing up what I'm saying between generous bites of his sandwiches.

Now he asks, "Tell me more about those in the 'believe-God-at-His-Word category."

I am only too happy to try. "All right, here goes. We believe the Bible to be infallible, inerrant, and therefore totally trustworthy and sufficient to teach the way of salvation and how to live a life of service to God. In other words, the Bible is authoritative to teach us what to believe and how to behave."

Tommy acts like I have fallen into his trap. "I've heard that it is necessary to have a governing body somewhere who tells you how to interpret the Bible and what you should do."

I know what he's getting at and try to choose my words carefully. "There are those who can help us better understand what the Bible teaches, like preachers—that's what I hope to be in Brazil. But no one person or organization can stand as an authority over the Bible as an interpretive body who alone wear the magic glasses, so to speak, to whom we must follow unquestionably. Scripture teaches us all to 'test them all; hold on to what is good.'[3] The Bible authenticates itself, proving itself to be true, without the need for any external authority to affirm it. And it has stood the test of time."

Tommy raises an eyebrow.

I try to reinforce what I have just said. "The Bible is a collection of sixty-six books written over a period of sixteen hundred years

---

[3] 1 Thessalonians 5:21

by some forty different human authors, most of whom never met each other. And although writing in either Hebrew, Greek, or Aramaic, they all wrote with the same objective: to reveal the person and work of Jesus Christ to the glory of God alone. The Bible is amazingly consistent with itself, historically and scientifically viable, perfectly explaining what we see all around us and even what lies within our own hearts. It has survived being tried and tested for the past two thousand years by some of the most brilliant minds on every continent."

I realize I'm speaking very fast and hope I'm not gabbling. I nibble my sandwich before continuing. "Many an empire has come and gone, but the Bible continues to shape the world as we know it. The full Bible has now been translated into seven hundred languages, and portions have been translated into over two thousand further languages! One hundred million copies of the Bible are sold each year—around six billion so far."

Tommy seems impressed, but that wasn't my intention.

"I appreciate your questions, Tommy, because it is essential for us to know if the Bible is reliable or not, as we cannot trust anyone completely. Everyone is wrong sometimes. Whereas some mislead for personal gain, others can be wrong unintentionally. Shockingly, we can even deceive ourselves! 'The heart is deceitful above all things and beyond cure. Who can understand it?'[4] That is why we must have an authority outside of ourselves which is not led astray by any one individual or organization which might manipulate it for their own ends, causing others to blindly follow, content that they have done the thinking for us. That's what happens in cults."

---

4   Jeremiah 17:9

Tommy has just about finished his sandwiches, while I have barely begun mine. The Land Rover is so steamed up that everything outside is a green blur. It's time to get back to work and for me to climb that scary tree once more. But I first want to reaffirm the confidence we can have in God's truth.

"The Christian faith is not a blind faith. It is built upon everything the Bible clearly reveals, that which God has declared and preserved for us to know. The Christian church and all we believe is 'built on the foundation of the apostles and prophets, with Christ Jesus himself as the chief cornerstone.'"[5]

I reach out to open the car door. Once outside the Land Rover, Tommy asks, "How do you know there will not be any more books inspired that might force you to modify your beliefs?"

That's not a simple question; I thought we were wrapping up this conversation. We walk as slowly as possible back to the tree, as I explain, "Jews in Jesus' day divided the Old Testament into three sections: the Law of Moses, the Prophets, and the Psalms (or wisdom books), which all speak of Jesus.[6] There is a warning not to add or take anything from the Law in the last of its five books.[7] There is also a warning sealing the five books of wisdom.[8] Now, bear with me. It's interesting how Malachi—the last book of the twelve books of prophesy which complete the Old Testament—sets the stage for what will follow in the New Testament. The very theme of that book is a warning that God has finally rejected the Jewish nation as a whole, including its sacrificial system of worship, because of

---

5 Ephesians 2:20
6 Luke 24:44
7 Deuteronomy 4:2; 12:32
8 Proverbs 30:5-6

the blasphemous way they were attempting to approach God. Yet, mercifully, God speaks of a 'treasured possession,'[9] God's people, comprising Jews and non-Jews (Gentiles), whom He would spare and speak to once more beginning with two 'messengers.'[10] These we believe to be John the Baptist[11] and Jesus.[12]

"Now to answer your question concerning why there will be no further revelation, the last book in the Bible, called Revelation, has a theme of finality—the consummation of all things, including the final judgment when Jesus returns. In fact, it has a seal upon its last page warning about adding or taking anything from it.[13] And no book since then, for two thousand years, has been accepted as inspired Scripture by biblical Christians. Some books which claimed this for themselves or had it attributed to them have since been proven to be forgeries and/or inconsistent with the sixty-six books that we already have and call the Bible."

We are now standing at the foot of the great tree. Tommy is shielding his eyes from the sun and studying its structure. After all, he is the expert tree surgeon. I wonder if I have said too much.

"Sorry for such a long answer, but you did ask. And I am glad you did. It is so important. Satan is always wanting to imitate God, to twist and to distort what He has done and said."

"Just one more question." Tommy has a cheeky sparkle in his eye as he says, "What would you say to the concept of a mean God

---

9   Malachi 3:17
10 Malachi 3:1; 4:5-6
11 Luke 1:11-17; Matthew 17:11-13
12 Hebrews 1:1-3
13 Revelation 22:18-19

in the Old Testament and a meek One in the New? And the idea of modifying Him to line up with our day?"

As I refuel my chainsaw, I affirm, "First, it is important to know that as God doesn't change, neither does His Word. What was true then is true now. Where there might not be direct answers to specific questions that we have, there are consistent principles throughout the Bible which are clear and that we may apply to any given situation, in whatever culture and century we find ourselves.

"Here's an example. God flooded the ancient world in Noah's day, killing every man, woman, and child, except for the family of Noah—eight in all—who survived by entering the ark that God commanded him to build.[14] But this wasn't mean; it was judgment. Later, it was the so-called meek Jesus Who spoke more about Hell and eternal punishment than any Old Testament prophet ever did, while still holding out the free offer of salvation to all who come to Him in repentance and faith. Repentance is a turning from sinful, selfish behavior—that which is contrary to God's character and commands—and turning to God in humble submission, seeking forgiveness and acceptance upon the merits of Jesus. Jesus illustrated this in the story of the prodigal son.[15] The apostle Paul also explained this to the philosophers of his day in Athens.[16] And he applies it to the Corinthians when he preaches, 'Godly sorrow brings repentance that leads to salvation and leaves no regret, but worldly sorrow brings death.'"[17]

I step into my harness and adjust the ropes. "We don't need to invent or edit what God has said to fit our transient common era. We

---

14 Genesis 6-9
15 Luke 15:11-32
16 Acts 17:16-34
17 2 Corinthians 7:10

just have to carefully and prayerfully seek to understand what God was saying to them there and then. Then we can begin to apply the very same teachings to us, here, now. This is how we can know what is true and how to understand and live by that truth. I couldn't go to Brazil to teach others the trustworthiness of the Bible if I didn't believe it myself."

Tommy nods slowly but still, frustratingly, gives nothing away. All the way through our conversation, it is hard to know where he stands on these matters. I remember his original line of questioning, which seemed to be tinged by doubt, yet underscored with a desire for certainty.

I start to climb up the tree, pulling the slack out of the ropes with my aching arms and stomach muscles. Before I am out of earshot, I venture to say one more thing. "Tommy, back in the Garden of Eden, Eve got into a conversation with Satan about whether God's Word was to be trusted.[18] Satan planted doubt in her mind by first misquoting God, then blankly denying the meaning of what He said, and finally, suggesting that somehow God was acting unfairly and holding back something good from her. Satan played on her healthy desire to want to be like God, until it became an unhealthy desire. She wanted to achieve it on her own terms, to satisfy her own pleasure."

I stop climbing to rest a second. "This is how we can expose every false religion and cult. We need the Bible because we need to hear what God's terms are for our own good and for His glory. We can only be truly happy when we know what pleases Him and obey Him out of love."

---

18 Genesis 3

The conversation ends for the afternoon as we set our sights on the branches hanging above us, but I have a feeling that the conversation is far from over.

Early the next morning, I call round to Tommy's house in order to set off together with him in his Land Rover. Now I meet his lovely wife for the first time. She calls me in to their rustic cottage. I sit at one end of a large, mahogany table in a cramped room that has a low, oak-beamed ceiling.

She says, "Tommy told me of your conversation yesterday. Isn't it great that we can trust God at His Word?"

I don't know what face I pulled, but it is sufficient for her to look at Tommy disapprovingly. "You did tell him, didn't you?"

"Tell him what?" Tommy smiles wryly, feigning ignorance.

She looks back at me. "We are Christians also. We believe everything the Bible teaches as God's Word." She smiles, knowing the mind games Tommy likes to play. "I think he was just testing you yesterday to see if you were genuine or not."

CHAPTER 2
The God Who Is

The following story includes excerpts from "The Plot: Ninja Turtle/Mortal Combat Star gets saved."[19]

Ever heard of Jeff Durbin? If you are under fifty, you may have without realizing it. I will let him introduce himself. "I was world champion. I played Johnny Cage, Night-wolf, Baraka in *Mortal Combat: the Live Tour*, and Michelangelo and Donatello for the *Ninja Turtles* franchise. I have been in movies, video games, television shows. I've traveled across the country and taught thousands of martial arts students . . . And then it all came crashing down."

This is how Jeff Durbin begins his testimony. He goes on to say:

> I wasn't raised in an explicitly Christian home. I wasn't raised under the hearing of the Gospel. I wasn't raised going to church every Sunday. I was raised with a basic understanding that there was this book that collected dust on a shelf. And that there was someone named Jesus Who died and rose again . . . And that was all I

---

19 "The Plot: Ninja Turtle/Mortal Combat Star gets saved," YouTube video, 17:55, Apologia Studios, February 6, 2016, https://www.youtube.com/watch?v=_9WhUtDNSPQ.

> knew. So, I grew up, and my passion was martial arts. I started Judo at four years old. I ended up going to Japan . . . I trained a lot, every day; that was my passion; that was my whole life . . . I was a national champion, won international championships. I was a world champion. I accomplished everything I wanted to in martial arts. I got five blackbelts. In some sense while I was young, that was my idol, that was what I worshipped.

By sixteen years old, Jeff Durbin was already owner of his own martial arts club, and it seemed like he had it made. So, what happened? What went wrong?

From Riches to Rags

He remembers settling down one evening with a TV dinner and watching a Billy Graham program, which introduced him to the basics of the Christian faith. Although he thought that he had a conversion experience, he admits that what he heard had no lasting effect upon his life, even though he began reading the Bible and going to church. He says:

> I had a problem. There was the church Jeff, the guy that everyone knew who had professed faith in Jesus. Then there was the Jeff that I was behind closed doors, with sexual relationships outside of marriage. I did what I wanted when I wanted . . . I was living a double life. There was the Christian Jeff, and there was the sinful,

do-as-I-please Jeff. I don't think I was even aware of the contradiction of my life.

At the age of twenty-one, he got married. But that didn't stop him continuing to live for himself and following the downward spiral into heavy drugs and alcohol usage to feed a crippling addiction that would take him to the brink of death. After two days of excess in Las Vegas, he remembers staggering around the streets alone in the early hours and clutching an ice bucket filled with alcohol, having already consumed some Ecstasy pills.

> I felt that God was chasing me. I sensed it . . . This is where God crushed my life. This one night, I had taken six tablets of Ecstasy. It was at the point that it was not working anymore. I had to take so much to even feel anything. It was three or four in the morning in a dark house at an after-party. I had this bottle of Vodka, and I'm just drinking it. I remember, all at once, that my whole body felt that it was on fire. I looked down at my hands and my arms. They were red—I mean, blood red . . . and I felt like my face was on fire . . . Ecstasy users know how you die from Ecstasy—basically cook yourself from the inside. You dehydrate; your heart stops. And I knew at this moment, that was what was happening.

He tried an ice bath, but his condition continued to worsen.

Lying wet and naked on my bed, I was high; I was hot; and I was dying. And I prayed. I said, "God, I know that this is because of my sin. I know, God, that You have the right to kill me . . . but please, just don't kill me yet. Please crush my life, destroy my life, and help me. Over." All of a sudden, my heart was beating normally. I was no longer hot. I was fine. I came out of this drunken, Ecstasy-laden stupor in an instant. Fine.

A Giant Leap in the Right Direction

Yes, Jeff had taken a giant leap in the right direction, but he will tell you himself:

It wasn't repentance. It wasn't even genuine. I just didn't want to die. About two to three weeks later, God crushed my life between six o'clock to noon, all in one day, all in one day. My phone was shut off; my electric was shut off; my water was shut off; I had an eviction notice on my door; they were repossessing my car; and the person I was working for at the time told me, "I'm not going to pay you. Sue me!" So, I'm left now in this apartment with total silence. And that was where God really started to speak with me through His Word. I knew that all I really had was God. I knew that it was me that had done this. It was all me. I wasn't simply an addict; I was a wretch. I was a sinner.

Jeff's wife was instrumental in leading him through the Scriptures to really understand the soul-saving message there that he had read before but never really understood. Then, as it began to penetrate his heart, he said, "'God, I'm turning to You now. Please forgive me. Please save me. Take over my life. You're the Boss. You tell me what to do. You run my life. You save me and take over my life." And that's when everything changed.

From Addict to Apologist

The drugs became a shameful memory of abuse on himself and those who loved him. Instead of idolizing and worshipping martial arts, he dedicated his time to knowing Who God really is. He presently helps to pastor a church in Arizona; he has a radio and television ministry; and he is often found outside of abortion mills and Mormon places of worship, trying to reach out to others with the Gospel that saved him and transformed his life.[20]

The Ontology (Being) of God

Jeff Durbin is also a popular speaker and public debater. The following section includes extracts taken from a debate in which he makes a defense for the existence of God against the claims of atheism:

> Our claim is that the triune God of Scripture exists. From a biblical and philosophical perspective, neutrality is a myth. Biblically, no one is neutral towards the triune God. Outside of a saving relationship with Jesus Christ, we are all fallen and in a hostile relationship with our Creator. And thus, the problem is not evidence for this

---

20 His varied ministry is in association with the church he helped found and now pastors called Apologia Church in Arizona—www.apologiachurch.com.

God, or lack of light; the problem is sin and suppression. We are holding down the truth, which is obvious to all of us.[21][22]

Now that's quite a bold way for Jeff to begin, and as we go on, you will see on what kind of a foundation this faith is built. Really, this is the study of ontology (the study of being). Either God *is*, or He *isn't*. If He *is*, can He be known? If so, Who is He, and what has He done? What is He doing? And what has He promised to do? Then naturally, what bearing should this have on us?

If He *isn't*—if God does not exist—then how could we be sure of that? And what bearing would that have upon us individually and for the human race at large? In fact, you will discover that holding to this second position, most commonly referred to as atheism (literally, "without God"), takes greater faith as you must hold to the belief that everything came out of nothing without intelligence, purpose, or design.

The Achilles' Heel of Atheism

This leaves the thoughtful atheist frustrated without evidence to support their claims—only a faith commitment that everything is a product of nothing going nowhere with no purpose. Inconsistently, no atheist actually lives like that; but instead, while denying the God-given dignity of what it is to be human as opposed to just a mutated

---

21 Romans 1:18-21
22 "Incredible: Christian vs. Atheist Debate (White & Durbin vs Clark & Ellis)," YouTube video, 1:55:09, Apologia Studios, October 9, 2019, https://www.youtube.com/watch?v=vx0rlVap194.

animal, they still demand human rights, desire justice, and make moral judgements. In other words, they live as if there was a purpose to life and desire to be favorably remembered after they die, even by a universe they claim doesn't care. This is why in relation to the atheists he was debating, Jeff said:

> Given our opponent's view of the world and commitments, this debate would be incoherent, meaningless, irrelevant, and wasteful. Why the descendants of highly evolved societies of bacteria would be exercising energy arguing for anything at all in this ultimately purposeless universe should be perplexing to all of us. According to them, we are stardust in an environment with no ultimate purpose, no ultimate meaning, no [absolute] good or evil, and we are the random results of evolutionary processes that did not have us in mind.[23]

If God *is,* how can we be sure of *Who* or *What* He is and not fall into the trap of worshipping a false god from someone else's—or even from our own—imagination? For that would be idolatry and would surely anger the true God, Who alone is worthy of all adoration and our humble service. Jeff is quick to say, "The claim of the triune God of Scripture is that He has revealed Himself to us in the created order and that His creation is constantly testifying to His existence, presence, and power. He has revealed Himself to each and every one of us to the degree that we are left without a defense or an apologetic for our turning away from Him in our denials of His existence."

---

23   Ibid.

He is referring to what God has *done* in creation to His first general revelation, which proves that He *is*.[24] Then to know *Who* He is, God has chosen to give us proof by what He has said, which is the Bible, His special revelation of Himself. Jeff confidently reminds us, "According to the Christian confession, God is a spirit,[25] infinite,[26] eternal[27] and unchangeable in His being,[28] wisdom,[29] power,[30] holiness,[31] justice,[32] goodness,[33] and truth.[34]"

Necessary Truth

Now, let us reason together. What would necessarily have to be true for God to be God? The very concept of God suggests a Supreme Being, "a being than which no greater can be conceived."[35] He would be the uncreated Creator of all things. If not, whatever created Him would be the supreme being. If uncreated, then He would have to be eternal. If there is *anything*, then there must always have been *something*. And that *something* would have to have intelligence by which to create and sustain all else. In fact, He would have to have all knowledge, as He could not create something that knew what He did not. And to know all things, He would always have

---

24 Psalm 19:1-4; Romans 1:18-31; Ecclesiastes 3:11
25 John 4:24
26 Jeremiah 23:24
27 Revelation 1:8
28 Malachi 3:6
29 Psalm 147:5
30 Colossians 1:6
31 Isaiah 6:3
32 Deuteronomy 32:4
33 Mark 10:18
34 John 14:6
35 St. Anselm, Archbishop of Canterbury, Chapter II, *Prosologion,* Accessed November 7, 2024.

to be everywhere. Otherwise, things could happen outside of His experience, and He would be dependent upon an external source to inform Him.

For God to be God, He must be all-powerful and not dependent upon or influenced by a power outside of Himself. If God had such an external dependency, that power would have an independent, eternal, and intelligent source sustaining it, another supreme being. But of course, there cannot be two supreme beings. This then rules out the possibility of all other religions and their accompanying holy books as authentic. The idea of there being one God and everyone in every other religion basically worshipping Him by other names and practices, as some propose, with many paths leading up the same mountain, is very naive.

Make a comparison yourself. Some claim one God, others many gods. Some claim that time is linear, others that it is circular. Some claim bodily afterlife; others deny it—and so on. Either all religions are wrong, as the atheists claim, or one is right. Therefore, God must be totally independent, self-existent, and self-sufficient, the uncaused Cause and Regulator of all things.

God Is the Standard

As such, God is the standard by which all else is measured, the embodiment of infinite perfection. Neither His power nor His knowledge could increase or decrease, for that would suggest imperfection. How could that which is perfect become more perfect? And how could One that is, in essence, perfect, unable to be influenced by outside forces, be the cause of His own imperfection?

This also affirms His immutability (the impossibility of change in God). "'I am the Alpha and Omega,' says the Lord God, 'who is, and who was, and who is to come, the Almighty'" (Rev. 1:8). This title is also attributed to Jesus in Revelation 21:6 and 22:13. This teaching is amazingly and succinctly summed up by God's own self-designated Name, "I AM" (Exod. 3:14), meaning, "I am who I am," or, "I will be what I will be." This is the title that Jesus also attributed to Himself a number of times in the book of John[36] and in Revelation.[37] "I the LORD do not change" (Mal. 3:6).

I apologize for the weightiness of the above paragraphs. But it is necessary to think these things through, especially as this is God's self-revelation—the God with Whom we have to do. Or otherwise stated, the God to Whom we are subject. As our Creator, He is the One "in [Whom] we live and move and have our being" (Acts 17:28). "In his hand is the life of every creature and the breath of all mankind" (Job 12:10). Any moment He could withhold our next breath or say to our heart, "Stop beating." We are not merely victims to random events, to time acting upon matter by chance, without design or purpose.

Universal Laws Confirm God's Existence

Jeff Durbin has more to say about how the fact that God *is* affects the way we all operate in the world: "All human experience depends upon the uniformity in nature, or the inductive principle that the future will be like the past."

---

36 John 4:26, 6:35, 8:12, 8:24, 8:58, 9:5, 10:7, 10:11, 10:36, 11:25, 13:19, 14:6, 15:1, 18:6
37 Revelation 1:17-18, 2:23, 21:6, 22:16

Let me explain. This principle of induction is essential for us to live ordered lives. Although this sounds complicated, we actually take this principle for granted: "that the future will be like the past." This would include the predictable effects of gravity, the properties of water being constant, the speed of sound being reliable, the unchangeableness of logic, etc. We presume that these realities in operation today will be as real tomorrow as they were yesterday. In fact, all scientific inquiries rely upon there being *uniformity* in the universe.

There are many examples of scientists through the last few centuries, perhaps Isaac Newton being prince among them, who believed in a Sovereign God Who created an ordered universe in which science is possible.

Now, at first glance what you are about to read may seem complicated, but don't be put off. It is actually quite wonderful when fully grasped. In an article called, "Newton: The Mechanical Universe," it states, "Newton combined deductive logic from a given premise with inductive reasoning from empirical observation and from the combination he derived a tentative premise known as a 'hypothesis' . . . This was how the laws of nature were thought to be discovered." Later on in the article, it is noted, "When he was twenty three[sic] years old, Newton used the process of induction to correlate the observations of Copernicus, Kepler, Bacon, Galileo, and Descartes and accomplished a synthesis of their works."[38]

---

38 "Newton: The Mechanical Universe," Holisticeducator.com, Accessed July 18, 2022, https://www.holisticeducator.com/newton.htm.

A Rational Mind and the Principle of Induction

Our use of the principle of induction—"that the future will be like the past"—gives us confidence that the tools we use operate in predicted ways, unless something is malfunctioning; that the same methods and calculations applied the same way in the same circumstances will have the same outcome. And if they don't, then perhaps something has been overlooked, miscalculated, or a more efficient or accurate method/calculation has been discovered.

And so, we use the principles of science to test and retest these once predicted and then observable outcomes to prove or disprove certain expectations. This can only be done effectively due to the principal of induction, the uniformity of nature, "that the future will be like the past."

We apply this idea of regularity when communicating with one another. God has given us minds that can understand language which has objective meaning and regulating laws of grammar and syntax. We all rely upon a given context to help us understand the way in which a word is being used. For example, the apostle John uses the word *world* seventy-eight times in his writings, while assigning at least ten different meanings to that word. We can understand what he is referring to by its context. Misunderstandings occur when the context is ignored or misinterpreted.

And when new words, idioms, and ideas enter into a language, for them to carry meaning and communicate intelligible thoughts, they must be connected to previously existing words and ideas (with objective meaning and regulating laws of grammar and syntax) which previously existed and which they may be replacing or advancing.

One more evidence relating to the principle of induction would be our ability to use and rely upon logic. An example is the law of non-contradiction. This affirms that two contradictory facts cannot both be true in the same sense, at the same time, and in the same relationship. No one could communicate reliably if this law was not commonly accepted.

Hard Questions Atheist Cannot Answer

Where do these laws and principles originate? Could they have randomly and spontaneously popped into existence one day or evolved slowly as a result of time and chance? Could nothing exploding into something, for no reason, without design or intelligence, really be the answer as the origin of all things? Could countless chance mutations in an undirected evolutionary process be responsible for the ordering of chaos? Can design evolve without a designer? Can intelligence be the product of non-intelligence?

Those who deny the triune Creator God of Christianity and instead hold to the Big Bang Theory must say, "Yes, it is possible," to at least one of those suggestions. Those who believe the universe (or even multiverse) to be eternal actually have a distorted and deficient God-concept, which does not come about from scientific research but from a position of faith. It is another religion which the whole contents of this book disputes.

Those who believe in the Big Bang Theory as a possible explanation for the beginning of life as we know it have a huge problem: the universe would have to *be* before it was. Something had to explode; and the natural laws and principles would have to be in operation before there was anything for them to act upon—which would certainly defy logic.

How would a semi-evolved law of gravity operate? Could there be somewhere in the universe where the law of non-contradiction doesn't yet exist? What if logic evolved into non-logic in, let's say, Russia one day? No satisfactory answer can be deduced from the theory of evolution. And to conclude that these questions are ridiculous only strengthens the case for the necessary and constant existence of the principle of induction (uniformity in nature).

These regulating universal laws point beyond themselves to an all-knowing and all-powerful Supreme Being Who not only created but Who also sustains His universe. Wouldn't this principle of induction deny the possibility of creation? For if everything that exists is just as it has always been in the past, does this not imply that the universe is eternal? And at the other end of history: doesn't this principle of induction rule out the possibility that one day there will be a Day of Judgment and, after that, a renewed Heaven and earth (as affirmed in Rev. 20:11-22:27)? Isn't everything just going to carry on predictably in every *tomorrow*, just like it did in every *yesterday*? No, no, and no.

First, let's give a negative refutation. These universal principles and laws are neither incidental, nor self-existent. The argument being made here is that those who hold to the theory of evolution as reason for our existence are unable to give a rational reason for them *being* in the first place.

Now, let's give a positive affirmation: God is the Source and Moderator of every principle and law at work in the universe. They either proceed from His very being (i.e., logic exists because God is logical) or were designed, set in motion, and are continually upheld by His power and knowledge and according to His good pleasure and purpose (i.e., the principle of induction).

What About 2 Peter 3:3-4?

Let us remind ourselves of what is stated there: "You must understand that in the last days scoffers will come, scoffing and following their own evil desires. They will say, 'Where is this "coming" he promised? Ever since our ancestors died, everything goes on as it has since the beginning of creation'" (2 Peter 3:3-4).

The objection above, put forth by scoffers against the biblical prophecy and promise concerning the return of Christ and His renewal of all things, actually affirms that this principle of induction and uniformity in nature were accepted and relied upon by the objectors: "'everything goes on as it has since the beginning of creation'" (2 Peter 3:4).

But what is being overlooked is the fact that God is able to act contrarily to these laws and principles that He has set in place if He so chooses. We are bound to operate according to them; He is not. Remember, God is the eternal, all-powerful, all-knowing, self-dependent Creator and Sustainer of all things, Who is also a Spirit and therefore unbound by either time, matter or space.

Admittedly, it is unusual for Him to act contrarily to these principles and laws; but when He does, we call such events "miracles." Interestingly, when someone attempts to deny the historicity of miracles, they often do so on the basis of the principle of induction and uniformity ordinarily found in nature.

Therefore, amusingly, the objection that the principle of induction somehow undermines the possibility of the supernatural turns in on itself by pointing to the uniformity that is otherwise observed in nature, which we have been arguing to the point that it proves that the triune God of Scripture is the one true God.

And it is He Who tells us that "by [His] word" He is able to overrule such principles and laws as He did in His judgment by water in Noah's day (2 Peter 3:5) and as He shall yet do when He shall finally judge the "present heavens and earth . . . [by] fire," "by the same word" (2 Peter 3:7).

Good, Evil: What's the Difference?

Now, let's move on to other consequences of worldview, whether one has belief in or denies the existence of God. Who determines what is considered moral and ethical?

Universally, it is believed that there is a concept of goodness. Most people who consider themselves secular still like to believe that they are basically a good person with good intentions. But what is the moral standard against which they measure themselves? They are forced to conclude that which is socially expedient, here and now.

And what about when social standards and expectations shift, as they so often do, and that which was once commonly accepted as good is now considered bad and what was considered bad is now accepted as good? They are left with no choice but to vilify those who were once heroes and to idolize yesterday's devils. Historically, certain ethnicities have been considered as sub-human—as less-evolved—and therefore do not have equal human rights. At the time, the majority in those societies believed it was acceptable. In many cultures, women and children are considered inferior in dignity and treated with less respect. Examine historical (and some current) law books in almost any nation to see examples of this. There have been devastating effects as a result—such as massacres, holocausts, wars, oppression, cruelty, and other great acts of injustice.

How then can the secularist speak of intrinsic goodness and complain of evil? Certainly, their adopted standard of majority rule fails to provide an ultimate reason why anything is good or evil. And they have no basis upon which to support the idea of human dignity. The Bible states that every human being is made in God's image, which, incidentally is not said of any animal (Gen. 1:26-27). As such, we share some of God's characteristics, although finite and corrupted by the Fall. The natural man can still perform acts of kindness, love, mercy, forgiveness, and so on. Everyone has a conscience, which counsels us to do what is right and which shames us if we do not act upon it. Although, if persistent, we can learn to quiet and even to silence this inner voice.

The Affects of the Fall and Moral Awareness

The Fall—and our inherent sinful condition—means that our truest motives are no longer pure and no longer exclusively for the glory of God nor for the good of our neighbor; naturally, our good behavior is incapable of performing a righteous act (that which is pleasing to God). If examined closely enough, what motivates us is simply the preservation of self and our own pleasure.

What many people fail to consider is that if goodness is a real concept—and it is—then it must proceed from One Who is altogether lovely, just, faithful, and true. A God Who was altogether bad or evil could not be the source of anything that was perfectly good, as it would undermine Himself, making Himself less than perfect—which no perfect being could do—as already considered. Neither could an altogether good God be the source of anything bad or evil, for the same reason.[39]

This confirms why ethical behavior—that which ought to be done—should be based upon the unchanging principles that God reveals in the Bible, from which we derive what is dignified, meaningful, beautiful, and true—that which aligns and conforms to God's good will and character to the praise of His glory (Eph. 1:3-14). It is also for our well-being that God so directs us to do what is right. From this, we get law and order, justice and peace. One obvious example can be found in the Ten Commandments: "'Honor your father and your mother, so that you may live long in the land the LORD your God is giving you'" (Exod. 20:12).

We are wise to willingly submit to God's directives, especially as it then follows that those who oppose the Divine standard and will are, by definition, acting immorally, unethically, and sinfully and are ultimately accountable to God, Who will judge them according to that same perfect standard: that being Himself.

In the meantime, people become increasingly lovers of self at the expense of their fidelity and families. The pursuit of selfish desires is harmful for everyone. Little by little, the very stitches of society

---

[39] A consideration of the origin of evil can be found in Appendix A, although you are advised to read the whole book first so that you may more fully appreciate it when you arrive there.

become unpicked and communities impoverished as fatherlessness, substance abuse, gambling, debt, and general lawlessness become commonplace. Is this not what we see reported every day in the news?

No biblical Christian would claim that atheists are incapable of understanding morality or acting ethically. But we are saying that the *concept* of morality cannot come out of the atheist worldview, as they have no absolute standard by which to measure what is or is not moral. When they live by moral guidelines, they are borrowing from the Christian worldview, which they then dilute with subjective and pragmatic decision-making, deceiving themselves into believing that if it *appears* to work and serve the common good, then it must be right. Pragmatism is lethal as a moral gauge. It inevitably leads to the collapse of community, to social suicide, to the culture of death.

Who is worthy of life and the pursuit of happiness? According to atheism and those holding to the theory of evolution, it is the fittest who, by *chance*, have evolved/progressed ahead of the rest, sufficiently enough to secure a place in tomorrow's world for their offspring. They, in turn, may elbow their way in line, as their forefathers did, to grab what they can, while they can, without any real purpose or choice, intent on amusing themselves to death.[40]

This is why it is so important to take note of how Jeff Durbin summarizes this consideration:

> God is good and is the standard of good. His laws reflect
> His own character and justice. [Therefore] emotional

---

40 In 1992, Roger Waters released a song called "Amused to Death," on an album by the same name, which says more on this point. And he, in turn, was inspired by the book *Amusing Ourselves to Death: Public Discourse in the Age of Show Business* by Neil Postman, published by Viking Penguin (1985).

appeals to suffering, pain and evil in the world, make sense, if the triune God of Scripture exists. They have absolutely no coherent place in the atheist's worldview. Every time atheists appeal to human value and dignity, they are stealing from [the Christian] worldview. Nature is not chaos, time, and chance acting on random matter and mutations. God is the Sovereign.[41]

May this reasoned defense and proclamation of Who God is also act as a warning to those who may claim to be a Christian but live as an atheist. Are you honestly living in obedience to serve this triune God or just to survive another day taking care of your own needs? Regardless of who we *claim* to be, what we truly believe will be evidenced by what we actually *do*. So, what are you doing? Whose purpose directs your life?

God is holy and must judge all that He has created—and will do so justly. Pause and think about this: "We must all appear before the judgment seat of Christ, so that each of us may receive what is due us for the things done while in the body, whether good or bad" (2 Cor. 5:10). One day, you will have a face-to-face with God. What will you say to Him? What will He say to you?

---

[41] "Incredible," ibid.

CHAPTER 3
The God Who Judges

The following chapter includes excerpts from Francis Chan, an evangelist and Christian author.[42][43][44]

> I know what people are teaching. This is just an accident. But this is insane . . . We are sitting on a ball that is spinning one thousand miles an hour. That's weird! Seriously. Did you ever think about it? A ball of water that spins at one thousand miles an hour—that's normal? And this ball of water that has a core that is somehow hot . . . [is] flying around a ball of fire that's 1.3 million times our size that doesn't spin that's ninety-three million miles away. And we go, "Yeah, it's a little hot today." That's insane! We are flying around a ball of fire at sixty-seven thousand miles an hour. Right now . . . And you and I are going, "Yeah, it's an accident." People say, "There's no purpose . . . " But God says in the Bible, "No, nothing is an accident."

---

42 BR Ministries, "Talking to Leaders and CEO's by Francis Chan," YouTube, September 11, 2017, video, 48:33, https://www.youtube.com/watch?v=Ms6t5mImcuc. =
43 BR Ministries, "Talking to High School Students - Francis Chan," YouTube, August 10, 2017, 32:24, https://www.youtube.com/watch?v=iuq7XxkCQ54.
44 BR Ministries, "Francis Chan Live 2017 - from Facebook," YouTube, July 9, 2017, 48:10, https://www.youtube.com/watch?v=MUd_-fUpDzI.

Francis Chan is an evangelist and Christian author, born in 1967 in America from Chinese descent. After coming to saving faith in Jesus in his teens, it wasn't long before he began a church in his house. Within fifteen years, that house church grew into a mega church of six thousand people! Then he left because he didn't believe that the mega church model was God's intention for His people. He left to do some humanitarian work for the glory of God and then concentrated on the house church model once more.[45] Francis continues:

> You are not here because He needs you to serve Him. That's exactly what it says: "he's not served by human hands, as if he needed anything. Rather, he himself gives everyone life and breath and everything else." Why? Why did He determine these things? "God did this so that they would seek Him and perhaps reach out for Him and find Him, though He is not far from any one of us."[46]

Revelation Through Tragedy

I don't know what's happening in your life. God uses the craziest circumstances. But whatever He uses, I'm telling you, it's worth it. It's worth it to know Him. It's what this life's about. Francis had a traumatic childhood, which certainly left its mark on him. He said:

---

[45] A house church is when someone opens up their home to be used for Christian gatherings where people meet, under the pastoral oversight of elders, to study the Bible, sing, and pray together with a view to reach out and impact their community, serving Christ by making Him known to others. This model allows for a strong emphasis upon Church as a family, as everyone can be more involved in each other's lives as they all exercise their God-given gifts.

[46] Acts 17:25, 27

My mum died when she gave birth to me. That's kind of crazy to not have a mum. Then my dad remarried, but after a few years, my stepmom got into a car accident. I was eight years old. She died. Then my dad got married again. But when I was twelve, he died of cancer. I don't care how much faith you have, when you go to bed with those images of their bodies being put down in the grave, you think, "What in the world just happened?" It just ends. Then what . . . Do I just end? Is there some point in which we just stop existing? That never sat well with me. I couldn't get it. I felt there was more. Then I read the Scriptures, and I got it. Okay. I thank Him all the time for the tragedies in my life . . . It made me depend on Him.

Have you reflected upon the tragedies in your life in that way? Have they taught you to depend on God? Have they given you a better bearing upon your place in this life? In society? In view of an almighty and Sovereign God?

"The Wrath of the Lamb"

Francis has more to say to provoke a response:

> The moment I see God I am going to be terrified. Like everyone else . . . The Bible says, "He dwells in unapproachable light."[47] It talks about one hundred thousand million angels bowing down worshipping Him. Even the angels cover themselves up because

---
47 1 Timothy 6:16

they don't feel worthy to look upon this Being. And we are all going to face Him any second. Any second we are all going to see Him . . . and it doesn't matter who you are. I think of the book of Revelation. "Then the kings of the earth, the princes, the generals, the rich, the mighty, and everyone else, both slave and free, hid in caves and among the rocks of the mountains. They called to the mountains and the rocks, 'Fall on us and hide us from the face of him who sits on the throne and from the wrath of the Lamb!' For the great day of their wrath has come, and who can withstand it?"[48] It's talking about Jesus, the Lamb. Normally, we talk about Jesus, "Oh yeah, yeah, Jesus. He's my Buddy, my personal Savior." Here it's talking about the end times. And the wrath of the Lamb is going to be so powerful, you've got the rich and you've got the slaves all hiding together, wishing the mountains would just fall upon them because they can't bear the sight of the Lamb of God.

Everyone's on the same page. You know, we're all going to face this God, and it's going to be so, so intense. And I wonder how many people really get serious about these things with you. Look, our life is a vapor. We are living in the craziest times right now.

The Demigod Deception

We will hear more from Francis a little later. I've just got to bring to our attention the fact that there are so many caricatures of God.

---

[48] Revelation 6:15-17

You've heard many, I'm sure. You may even have taken one of them to heart and be holding on to it right now, possibly without realizing it doesn't agree with God's self-revelation of Who He is.

One of the first misconceptions I saw about God as a grandfather on a cloud was portrayed on TV, although it wasn't directly supposed to be God. Here's a clue: "Mork calling Orson; come in Orson. Mork calling Orson . . ."[49] Have you come across the American sitcom, *Mork and Mindy*? Officially, both Mork and Orson were from another planet, with Mork on a mission reporting back to his superior Orson on a regular basis, informing him of how life functioned on Earth— or something like that. They were both reliant on each other for purpose and information and moral support.

Some people are guilty of praying to God like Mork would talk with Orson—as if to tell Him stuff that He may not otherwise know and helping Him to better understand how life is functioning on Earth. Although Orson is definitely the superior authority figure, he is still evolving by adding to his knowledge and, therefore, is dependent upon his inferior.

In recent years, there has been an explosion of demigod or superhuman stories that dominate the silver screen. These are superhero films that have grown out of the comic craze that, in turn, grew out of a need for optimism in the American psyche in the 1940s. The Great Depression and the Second World War were coming to a close, although no one knew that for sure. People yearned for good-triumphing-over-evil stories—the little guy being protected or becoming the big guy and providing protection for other little

---

49 Garry Marshall, Joe Glauberg, and Dale McRaven, *Mork and Mindy*, Paramount Television, 1978-1982.

guys. That's basically it. These heroes share our flaws, our prejudices, our passions but are just a bit more impressive than we are. Basically, they are super versions of ourselves. They are who we wish we could be, if only . . . They inspire, give purpose, offer hope, and provide distracting entertainment. But this isn't new.

It is all a rehashing of Greek mythology. Centuries ago, people imagined that the gods were really just like us but a bit bigger, more clever, and stronger. While at the same time, when it came down to it, they were fickle and whimsical, sometimes heartless, sometimes moral, yet dependent upon humans to empower them. They thrived on "hero-worship." In return, it was believed they rewarded people with their divine assistance to ease their miserable lives. The needs of the people gave both them and their *gods* purpose for today and hope for tomorrow.

Meanwhile, the One and only true God needs nothing and no one. His purpose is not to serve us, like some genie in a bottle. Just rub your hands together in prayer and read from your wish list. Instead, God gives us *our* ultimate purpose, which is to serve *Him*.

Megalomaniac? Or Just MEGA?

When I was in my teens, I was very disturbed to hear someone I worked with ask, "Don't you think that God is a megalomaniac? Surely, if anyone else made something purely to worship Him, we would call that person arrogant." I confess I didn't know how to answer at the time. I knew that it was true God had all power and demanded worship from His creatures, as taught throughout the Bible. But I couldn't articulate an answer to the objection from my colleague. I can now, however. And the answer is not difficult to comprehend: God is not like us.[50] God is not a human being; He is not like us (Num. 23:19). He is Divine. There are billions of *human* beings, but there is just one *Divine* Being.[51] We are the creatures; He is the Creator. This goes a long way to understanding why God often doesn't do things how we want them done and why many prayers seem to go unanswered. We don't realize the danger we are in if we refuse Him the worship that He is due. Yes, He is worthy "'to receive power and wealth and wisdom and strength and honor and glory and praise'" (Rev. 5:12). We don't add to those qualities as if their source originated with us and that He somehow needs our contribution. Yet as we meditate upon Who He has revealed Himself to be, we ought to respond with heartfelt expressions of admiration, gratitude, humility, awe, and wonder. This is true worship (worth-ship). He needs nothing from us, while we are totally dependent upon Him for everything. He determines the rules and, as Judge, has the final word. He determines what is moral and immoral, right and wrong, and punishes or rewards accordingly.

God is "holy, holy, holy" (Isa. 6:3; Rev. 4:8); and He cannot do anything that would compromise what He is. Therefore, we must be holy to draw near to Him. Sin is abhorrent to Him. Tragically, we have all failed to meet that standard: "For all have sinned and fall short of the glory of God" (Rom. 3:23).

The truest sense of the English word *holy* (as the theologian R.C. Sproul used to teach) is best understood as an adjective for God. Every one of God's attributes is intrinsically holy. It goes way beyond simply

---
50 Cf. Jeremiah 10:6; Isaiah 55:8-11; 1 Samuel 15:29; Psalm 50:16-21
51 Cf. Isaiah 40-46

separate and *pure*. The closest English word we have to describe God's holiness is "other." God is *Other*. He transcends all that He has made. He exists outside of time and space, eternally separate from it and independent of it. This is what makes the incarnation of Jesus, the eternal Son of God and the second Person in the Godhead so mind-blowing and necessary for our salvation.

The Judge of All the Earth

Let's return to Francis Chan, who brings home the reality of the situation:

> All that matters is that there is a holy God in heaven, and He's watching right now. And I could die any moment. [Chan takes a deep breath.] That breath, was from God. [He does it again.] God gives breath to me, and any moment He can stop it. You know what? This God is a holy God, an awesome God. You are breathing right now because of Him. Yeah, I know, we live in a world right now where everyone says, "He can't judge me for this. He can't judge me for that." He can judge you for anything. He does what He wants.
>
> You know, we mask everything. Noah's Ark—isn't that cute? Let's paint it in our kid's nursery. Do you realize . . . what the story was all about? God killed everyone! Did you paint everyone drowning in the nursery? This God is free to do whatever He wants. He gives, and He takes away. He has all authority. Look, everyone is going to stand before Him. You are going to stand before that God. Even Isaiah, the prophet, the moment he saw

The God Who Judges

God he goes, "That's it! He's going to kill me!" John, the beloved disciple in Revelation chapter one, when he sees Jesus in His glorified state . . . who had the most intimate relationship with Jesus . . . when he sees Jesus, after He rose from the dead, after Jesus went back to Heaven . . . John is in awe of His glory . . . The moment he saw Him, he fell over like a dead man.

Understand! That's what's about to happen! There is a perfect God . . . Who has every right to judge us . . . He punishes as He sees fit. He punishes. Not me. And I do believe that that God is also a God of mercy and love, which blows my mind to think that He wanted to show one act of love that just surpasses every other act of love on earth. "Watch this, I will take my one and only Son . . . "—and as a father I get that—"and I'm going to watch Him suffer to pay for your crimes . . . " That's not all, He rose from the dead three days later to show, "Look. I am who I said I am." And He says, "Look. You can be forgiven for everything, if you believe that that actually happened. Not only that, I'm going to put [my] Spirit in you so you can understand these spiritual things . . . to know Him, to take on the mind of Christ. That's it. It's a simple story.

And we will explore this story further through the lives and ministries of some other objects of God's mercy. Hold tight.

CHAPTER 4
The God to Be Feared

The following chapter is from excerpts from Jonathan Edwards, one of the greatest preachers to have lived.

Imagine you had ten siblings, all girls and each six feet or taller! His father once quipped, "I have sixty foot of daughters."[52] Jonathan Edwards (October 5, 1703-March 22, 1758) was the only boy among eleven children. He was born and served mostly in the British colony of Massachusetts and is remembered as a revivalist preacher, philosopher, author, and theologian. Many consider Jonathan Edwards as the greatest ever American theologian. Although as he was of Welsh descent and lived in the British colonies, that would technically make him British.

"Happified"

Most commonly, there is an unfair caricature that he was little more than a "fire-and-brimstone preacher." He only preached about God's wrath and judgment. Yet in reality, he had a very gentle spirit, never shouting or showing aggression when he preached. On the contrary, he talked quietly and with a thoughtful and instructive tone. He desired

---

52   Douglas A. Sweeney, *Jonathan Edwards and the Ministry of the Word* (Downer's Grove: InterVarsity Press, 2009).

simply to lead people to realize their great dependence upon the grace of God. And the most common descriptive words he used in his sermons were "joy," "sweetness," "delight," and "happified." What a great word—to be made happy! This was Edward's lifelong quest—to explore for his own soul and to teach others through his ministry how it is possible to be truly happy—a quest that didn't begin with him, of course.

Like most English-speaking children of his day, Edwards was brought up on the Westminster Shorter Catechism.[53] The first question was, "What is man's primary purpose?" The answer: "Man's primary purpose is to glorify God and to enjoy Him forever." Augustine wrote, "Thou hast made us for thyself, O Lord, and our heart is restless until it finds its rest in thee."[54]

Edwards wrote:

> The doctrine of God's sovereignty is very often appeared as an exceeding pleasant, bright and sweet doctrine to me . . . God Himself is the great good, which the redeemed are brought to the possession and enjoyment of by redemption. He is the highest good, and the sum of all that good that Christ purchased. God is the inheritance of the saints. He is the portion of their souls. God is their wealth, treasure, their food, their life, their dwelling place, diadem and their everlasting honor and glory.[55]

Do you share that high view of God?

---

53 Written in 1646 by the Westminster Assembly, the catechism is comprised of 107 doctrinal questions and answers designed to encourage people to have a solid biblical understanding of the Christian faith.
54 Augustine, *Confessions*, transl. F.J. Sheed (London: Penguin Classics, 2008).
55 George Marsden, *Jonathan Edwards, A Life* (New Haven: Yale, 2003).

The God to Be Feared

The Sermon That Rocked the World

Then, there is the sermon—the one that rocked the world of Edwards' day, the one that even after nearly three hundred years is still considered by many to be one of the greatest ever preached in the English language. The social backdrop was one of political and civil unrest, spurred on by poverty and injustice, high infant mortality, sickness, and death, which were all daily realities. Life was tough. It was impoverished and embittered further as the fittest trampled the weak to lay claim to the dream of prosperity from the *new* world. The masses were left choking in the smog, limping along with nothing but a survivalist mentality, bewildered and disillusioned—perhaps not so different from our day. It was in this context that Edwards preached his world-famous sermon, "Sinners in the Hands of an Angry God," in Enfield, Connecticut, on July 8, 1741.

Oliver Wendell Holmes, an associate justice of the U.S. Supreme Court from 1902 to 1932, described this sermon as "barbaric." Without any justification, American author Mark Twain (1835-1910) called Edwards "a drunken lunatic." While the Welsh preacher D. Martyn Lloyd-Jones contended that "Puritanism[56] reached its fullest bloom" in Edwards.

Are you brave enough to be confronted by excerpts from that sermon? It was used of God to help ignite a spiritual awakening of souls, with an influence that crossed the Atlantic to England and beyond. Prepare to examine your own spiritual state, to see yourself as God sees you.

---

56 Puritanism took root in Europe in the sixteenth century, really following on from the necessary schism between Roman Catholic and Protestant Christians. They sought to transform society by applying biblical principles to civil law and order and lead by a godly example.

Can We Deceive Ourselves?

The biblical text Edwards set out to expound was, "In due time, their foot will slip" (Deut. 32:35). The warning was originally for those who followed Moses through the wilderness from slavery to freedom around thirty-five hundred years ago. They were the first audience to hear this warning and the first to neglect it. Despite already receiving much common grace[57] from God and being the generation that witnessed more miracles than any other, still, few took the warning seriously. Will you?

Shockingly, early on in his sermon Edwards says:

> There is nothing that keeps wicked men at any one moment out of hell, but the mere pleasure of God . . . They are already under a sentence of condemnation to hell. They do not only justly deserve to be cast down thither, but the sentence of the law of God, that eternal and immutable rule of righteousness that God has fixed between Him and mankind, is gone out against them, and stands against them; so that they are bound over already to hell. "He that believeth not is condemned already." The wrath of God burns against them, their damnation does not slumber; the pit is prepared, the fire is made ready, the furnace is now hot, ready to receive them; the flames do now rage and glow. The glittering sword is whet, and held over them, and the pit hath opened its mouth under them.

---

[57] "Common grace" is common because it is received by most people, most of the time; such as food, family, sunshine, rain, air, and so forth—grace being undeserved, a gift from God, a demonstration of His goodness.

Okay, timeout. Let's just catch our breath. Really? Hell? These days, we are discouraged from even uttering that word in polite society. Could a good God create a literal place called Hell? Does He threaten to cast people into it for eternity, forever and ever without end, without the possibility of annihilation, escape, or parole?

It must be understood that, as already considered, God is altogether holy and eternal. While all our sins, the wrong that we have thought, spoken and acted upon, are offenses against Him personally.[58] Our sin is hatred toward God, an attempt to undermine His Sovereign right to govern His universe according to His own pleasure and will. Once a sin is committed, there is nothing we can do either here on earth or in Hell to pay for a single offense. We cannot satisfy God's justice. And what's more, what makes you think that people stop sinning in Hell? There is no working of the Spirit of God in their afterlife to bring about true repentance. Therefore, the terrible consequences of sin are eternal.[59]

God is good and just; He cannot abide with sinners and wink at their offenses as if it were nothing. We would expect a human judge to judge justly, particularly if there was an offense committed against us or against someone we love. How much more should we expect "the Judge of all the earth [to] do right?" (Gen. 18:25).

Edwards continues:

---

[58] To better understand this concept, read 2 Samuel 11 (the crime), then Psalm 51 (the confession).

[59] Consider these texts soberly, in their proper context; mindful that where symbolic language is utilized, the reality is more, not less, extreme. Realities which can only begin to be fathomed through picture language: Isaiah 66:22-24, Daniel 12:1-2, Matthew 18:6-9, Matthew 25:31-46, Mark 9:42-48, 2 Thessalonians 1:5-10, Jude 7-13, Revelation 14:9-11 and 20:10-15. This is why the Gospel message is so urgent!

It is no security to wicked men for one moment, that there are no visible means of death at hand. It is no security to a natural man, that he is now in health . . . Unconverted men walk over the pit of hell on a rotten covering, and there are innumerable places in this covering so weak that they will not bear their weight, and these places are not seen. The arrows of death fly unseen at noon-day; the sharpest sight cannot discern them. God has so many different unsearchable ways of taking wicked men out of the world and sending them to hell . . . Almost every natural man that hears of hell, flatters himself that he shall escape it; he depends upon himself for his own security; he flatters himself in what he has done, in what he is now doing, or what he intends to do . . . But the foolish children of men miserably delude themselves in their own schemes, and in confidence in their own strength and wisdom; they trust to nothing but a shadow.

Beware of "Vain Dreams"

Then Edwards imagines a conversation with those who once thought likewise but are now in Hell. This is what they might say:

No, I never intended to come here: I had laid out matters otherwise in my mind . . . I thought my scheme good. I intended to take effectual care; but it came upon me unexpected . . . it came as a thief: Death outwitted me: God's wrath was too quick for me. Oh, my cursed foolishness! I was flattering myself and pleasing myself with vain dreams of what I would do hereafter; and

The God to Be Feared   55

when I was saying, peace and safety, then sudden destruction came upon me.

Now, Edwards applies this to those willing to listen:

> Thus all you that never passed under a great change of heart, by the mighty power of the Spirit of God upon your souls; all you that were never born again,[60] and made new creatures, and raised from being dead in sin . . . are in the hands of an angry God. However you may have reformed your life in many things, and may have had religious affections, and may keep up a form of religion in your families and closets, and in the house of God, it is nothing but his mere pleasure that keeps you from being this moment swallowed up in everlasting destruction . . . The God that holds you over the pit of hell, much as one holds a spider, or some loathsome insect over the fire, abhors you, and is dreadfully provoked: His wrath towards you burns like fire; He looks upon you as worthy of nothing else, but to be cast into the fire; He is of purer eyes than to bear to have you in His sight; you are ten thousand times more abominable in His eyes, than the most hateful venomous serpent is in ours . . . it is nothing but His hand that holds you from falling into the fire every moment. It is to be ascribed to nothing else, that you did not go to hell the last night; that you were [allowed] to awake again in this world, after you closed your eyes to sleep.

Some may be thinking that Edwards was just a man of his times and that this forceful speaking does not belong in our times, that we are simply to love people into the kingdom of God. But please pause to think about what he is saying; for as shocking as his warnings and descriptions are, they are not so different from what Jesus Himself said. Edwards goes on to quote Luke 12:4-5 in his sermon, which says, "And I say unto you, my friends, be not afraid of them that kill the body, and after that, have no more that they can do. But I will forewarn you whom you shall fear: Fear Him, which after He hath killed, hath power to cast into hell: yea, I say unto you, fear him" (Authorized KJV).

Once in Hell, God's mercy, grace, patience, and love will not be within reach. Edwards affirms this by then quoting Ezekiel 8:18:

> [God] will have no compassion upon you . . . Nothing shall be withheld, because it is so hard for you to bear. "Therefore will I also deal in fury; mine eye shall not spare, neither will I have pity; and though they cry in mine ears with a loud voice, yet I will not hear them" (Ezekiel 8:18). Now God stands ready to pity you; this is a day of mercy; you may cry now with some encouragement of obtaining mercy. But when once the day of mercy is past, your most lamentable and dolorous cries and shrieks will be in vain. It is everlasting wrath . . . Oh, who can express what the state of a soul in such circumstances is! All that we can possibly say about it gives but a very feeble, faint representation of it; it is inexpressible and inconceivable: for "who knows the power of God's anger?"

A Divine Invitation

Among Edward's closing provocative words, are these:

> Let every one [sic] that is out of Christ, now awake and fly from the wrath to come. Jesus Himself invites you, "'Come to Me, all you who are weary and burdened and I will give you rest'" (Matt. 11:28). Wow! What a promise! You may be weary from your resistance against God, your rebellion, your exposure to your temptations and willful life of sinning. You may be burdened by your attempts at keeping the law of God and the traditions of men . . . stricken by a conscience riddled with guilt and shame, confirming that your best efforts are insufficient. To you, Jesus says, "'Come to Me'" (Matt. 11:28).

Trust that He is sufficient to save you to the uttermost—yes, to save you from Hell but more than that. He wants to save you for Heaven to bring you into a right relationship with Himself, now and forever, by grace alone as He has done it all. Oh, to know Jesus is to know joy immeasurable. To be happified!

CHAPTER 5
The God Who Pursues

Martin Luther was born in Germany in 1483 to a well-to-do family. His father had high hopes that he might become a lawyer. Even in his early teens, he earned the nickname the Philosopher because of his debating skills.

Pride Comes Before a Fall

But a lightning bolt struck near him when he was riding to university. In his own words, he cried out, "Besieged by the terror and agony of sudden death." "Help me, St. Anne! And I will become a monk!"

Well, he survived, gave all his possessions away, and joined a monastery, much to his father's embarrassment and disappointment. Instead of enjoying a prestigious career and the comforts that kind of life affords, Luther immediately and completely dedicated himself to an ascetic lifestyle of self-neglect. His fasting and other attempts to tame the flesh took him to the point of death many times. And his hours and hours of daily confession to the priest in charge exhausted others to distraction. Later, he commented, "If anyone could have earned heaven by the life of a monk, it was I."

By good works and religious observance, which far exceeded everyone around him, Luther hoped his *moral* behavior would make him acceptable to God. His heart-cry was to be considered *righteous*, which is to say, to attain a right-standing before God, justified, innocent.

Maybe God used that lightning bolt to knock Martin from the "high horse" of his lofty lifestyle. Nothing Luther could do brought peace to his soul. Instead, he felt wretched, plagued by his guilt and shame, knowing that his good works were not good enough. I wonder if the words of Isaiah added to his troubled mind: "All of us have become like one who is unclean, and all our righteous acts are like filthy rags; we all shrivel up like a leaf, and like the wind our sins sweep us away" (Isa. 64:6).

What Do You Do with Your Guilt?

What efforts have you made in your life to get right with God? What do you do with your guilt? What, or who, are you relying on for peace with God?

Still in his early twenties, Martin Luther went to Rome. On arrival, he knelt, with hands raised, and said, "Hail to thee, holy Rome! Thrice holy for the blood of the martyrs shed here." Then he went on to visit the graves of forty-six popes and the cemeteries of eighty thousand martyrs. He also paid a visit to the Scala Sancta, which means "holy stairs." They are so called because it was believed that Jesus had ascended them to be interrogated by Pontius Pilate the night before His execution. It is taught that St. Helena brought the twenty-eight white marble steps from Jerusalem to Rome in the fourth century and that all who ascend them on their knees, praying the Lord's prayer (Matt. 6:9-13) on each step, will be the cause of the release of a soul from purgatory.[61] But when Luther, bleeding and bruised, reached the top, he felt as cold and distant from God as ever, and said, "Who knows if it is true?"[62]

Captivated by a Single Phrase

Nearly a decade later, while teaching through the Psalms for a second time, Luther wrote:

> I had confidence in the fact that I was more skillful, after I had lectured in the university on St. Paul's epistles to the Romans, to the Galatians, and the one to the Hebrews. I had indeed been captivated with an extraordinary ardor for understanding Paul in the Epistle to the Romans . . . but a single [phrase] in Chapter 1, "In [the gospel] the righteousness of God is revealed," had stood in my way. For I hated that word, "righteousness of God." . . . Though I lived as a monk without reproach, I felt that I was a sinner before God

---

61 Purgatory is a mythical place, somewhere between Hell and Heaven, where people who die believing in Christ Jesus as Lord and Savior may work hard and be punished sufficiently to complete what is necessary for their purging/cleansing from sin in preparation for Heaven. It is a doctrine that was neither taught nor believed by anyone anywhere before the twelfth century. And there is certainly no passage in the Bible which teaches it. Quite the contrary, God clearly reveals that, "People are destined to die once, and after that to face judgment" (Heb. 9:27). Consider the apostle Paul's confidence to die in Phil. 1:20-24 and in 2 Cor. 5:1-10, neither of which speak about an intermediate state. This is a confidence that can be shared even by new converts, saved from a wicked background, having done nothing to earn any favor with God. This was illustrated when the repentant, dying thief on a cross, by the side of Jesus, was assured, "Truly I tell you, today you will be with me in paradise" (Luke 23:43).

62 Martin Brecht and James Schaaf, *Martin Luther: His Road to Reformation 1483-1521, Vol. 1* (Minneapolis: Fortress Press, 1981), 103.

with an extremely disturbed conscience . . . I did not love, yes, I hated the righteous God who punishes sinners, and secretly, if not blasphemously, certainly murmuring greatly, I was angry with God, and said . . . [is it] not enough, that miserable sinners, eternally lost through original sin, are crushed by every kind of calamity by the law of the decalogue,[63] without having God add pain to pain by the gospel . . . threatening us with His righteousness and wrath?! Thus I raged with a fierce and troubled conscience.[64]

Gate to Paradise

What was Martin Luther's problem? What was he really "raging" against? This was the idea of a holy God Who would not, could not, accept anyone into His presence who was not altogether just: perfect and without sin. For Luther knew his own heart enough to know that he had fallen short of that mark and broken the Law, and all that awaited him was to be condemned and banished for eternity to Hell. And there was nothing he could do about it.

But God graciously, though gradually, helped Martin Luther to understand that for the Gospel to be truly seen for what it is—good news—it is necessary to meditate upon God's holy Law, His perfect standard portrayed in all the Old Testament, especially in the Ten Commandments. Yes, this painfully draws attention to our own deficiencies and failure to meet this standard. But then, before we despair completely, God reveals His Son Jesus to us, Who alone can

---

63 This refers to the Ten Commandments of God given to Moses, found twice in Scripture in Exodus 20 and Deuteronomy 5.
64 R.C. Sproul and Stephen J. Nichols, eds., *The Legacy of Luther* (Franklin: Reformation Trust Publishing, 2016).

fulfill the Law perfectly, as He was without sin (Gal. 3:22-24; 1 Peter 2:22; Heb. 4:15). That is why only His sacrificial death could pay the penalty for our sin on the cross (Rev. 5).

Finally, after a tortuous, dark season, Luther saw the light of this truth, which flooded his heart with peace. And may it do the same for you, too, to know that those for whom Christ came to save are given saving faith to believe that we may seek salvation in *His* name and be accredited with *His* righteousness, the very righteousness of God, as if it were ours to begin with (2 Cor. 5:21). And it is by this faith, trusting in Christ's finished work and not in our own, that the Christian lives. "The righteous will live by faith" (Rom. 1:17; Hab. 2:4; Gal 3:11; Heb. 10:38).

Hear the relief in Luther's own words:

> At last, by the mercy of God, meditating day and night, I gave heed to the context of the words, namely, "In [the Gospel] the righteousness of God is revealed, as it is written, 'The just shall live by faith.'" Here I felt that I was altogether born again and had entered paradise itself through open gates. There a totally other face of the entire Scripture showed itself to me . . . that is what God does in us, the power of God, with which He makes us wise, the strength of God, the salvation of God, the glory of God. And I extolled my sweetest word with a love as great as the hatred with which I had before hated the word, "righteousness of God." Thus that place in Paul [in the letter to the Romans] was for me truly the gate to paradise.

And you, too, are invited to walk through that "gate to paradise," trusting in Christ Jesus alone.

Connecting the Dots

You may have noticed a connection between our chapter three, with the contemporary words of Francis Chan highlighting our need for humility in light of God's holiness, followed by chapter four's focus on Jonathan Edwards' words two centuries earlier highlighting our very great danger if we ignore the salvation offered us by our just Judge. Then in this chapter, we traveled back two more centuries to witness Luther's liberation from relying upon his own good works to the perfect and finished work of Christ.

Now, as we end this middle section of the book, let us take a giant leap back even further to six thousand years ago to our first parents to see how all this began with a question.

Do you know what the first question was that God asked in the Bible? "Where are you?" (Gen. 3:9). God doesn't ask anything because He doesn't know the answer. Remember, He is omniscient. When God asks questions in the Bible, it is to help the one who is being asked and those of us listening in to meditate upon and learn from the answer He gives.

To whom was God first asking this pertinent question? To Adam. Why? Where was he?

Obey and Live, Disobey and Die

God had said to him, "You are free to eat from any tree in the garden; but you must not eat from the tree of the knowledge of good and evil, for when you eat from it you will certainly die" (Gen. 2:16-17). Simple. One commandment—just one—which was the pattern of all others to come. Obey Me and live, or disobey Me and die!

The God Who Pursues

Adam and Eve had all of paradise to feast upon, including the tree of "eternal life," no less. And although Adam was not the first to eat of the forbidden tree "of knowledge of good and evil," he was the silent partner while Eve was being deceived by the serpent, who was being used by Satan to plant seeds of doubt in their minds. Then Adam, without hesitation, took the fruit from his wife's hand and "ate it" (Gen. 3:6). Now, they were both guilty, and their shame was expressed through their awareness that they were naked before an all-seeing God. So what did they do? They "sowed fig leaves together and made coverings for themselves" (3:7). Had they thought that was a sufficient covering, why did they hide when they "heard the sound of the LORD God as He was walking in the garden in the cool of the day" (3:8)?

Then comes that weighty question from God Himself: "Where are you?" So, where were they? Hiding. Their situation was pitiful as they huddled together "among the trees of the garden" (3:8) with their fig-leaf coverings peeling away. They had *tried* and failed to put things right. Now, there was nothing for them to do but to hide and hope that God wouldn't find them, while they feared that He would sooner or later.

"I was afraid," Adam said (3:10). And he had every reason to be afraid. Thinking they knew better than God had led to disobedience. These rebels were now under the death sentence of God Almighty, their Creator and just Judge. Their best efforts to correct the situation had failed; they needed saving!

The clock had begun to tick down to the day of their death. Surely over and over in their minds God's warning was echoing: "When you eat from [the tree of knowledge of good and evil] you will certainly die" (2:17). Why had they listened to Satan who had possessed the serpent and hissed the words, "You will not certainly die" (3:4)? That was the very first lie that the Bible records and was spoken by the one who would later be referred to as "the father of lies" (John 8:44). Satan is also the father of doubts, as he dared to question the veracity of God's Word when he asked, "Did God really say . . . " (Gen. 3:1), a strategy that Satan has been using ever since to encourage people to doubt God's words.

The Fullness of Life

Now, with nothing but love and compassion, I ask you, even as God asked Adam, "Where are *you*?" Where have your attempts at good works and your pursuit for peace and happiness led you? What fig leaves have you spent your lifetime weaving together as a covering for your own guilt? You know in your heart of hearts that if your self-made covering was sufficient, then you would not be hiding from your faithful Creator. You would not be afraid.

God wanted Adam and Eve to consider how they were outside of fellowship with Him. Yet, mercifully, God had gone looking for them. They deserved to die. And they would die. But God had a plan. And this plan involved restoring them back into fellowship with Him through the redemptive work of the Last Adam, Jesus Christ.[65]

The reason why you are reading this book is because God has come looking for you, too. And guess what? He found you. As God's enemy, you have broken His Law; therefore, you also are under a

---

[65] Study 1 Corinthians 15:45-58 and Romans 5-6 to better understand this significance.

Divine death sentence. But God has a plan (Rom. 3:21-26). Jesus said, "I have come that they may have life, and have it to the full" (John 10:10). Eternal life—you may be surprised to learn it is a whole lot more than merely time without end.

I invite you to read on.

CHAPTER 6
The God Who Is Merciful

The following chapter features Little Richard (1932-2020), who is best known as an American singer, songwriter, and musician. He died, triumphantly in Christ, on May 9, 2020, while I was writing this chapter. Here, I have taken quotes from a recording that can be found online.[66]

"My name is Little Richard. I'm the rock-and-roll singer that you've heard about through the years. I'm the one who made 'Long Tall Sally,' 'Good Golly Miss Molly,' 'Rip It Up,' . . . 'Hey Lucille,' 'Keep A-Knockin,'' 'The Girl Can't Help It.'"

Some of you might be asking, "Am I still reading the same book?" Bear with me. You are in for a surprise. There is an amazing lesson we can learn from the self-proclaimed "Architect of Rock and Roll," and it's all about the mercy of God.

A Deal With the Devil

Much has been made of Little Richard's immeasurable influence upon the rock-and-roll scene during a career which lasted more than

---

66 Adelfred, "Little Richard—Little Richard's Testimony," YouTube, 2011, Radio Broadcast, 5:31, https://www.youtube.com/watch?v=l3jktkVg3lU.

half a century! He made such a big splash in the 1950s that his wave of influence left nowhere high and dry in the '60s. Early in that decade, Jimi Hendrix was a little-known guitarist in his band; James Brown was one of his backing singers; and the Beatles were his warm up act, as were the Rolling Stones, before any of them were famous enough to headline their own big shows.

Little Richard was a natural born glamor-performer who wore mirrored sequins, jewels, makeup with flamboyant hairstyles—all which framed his shrill and wildly passionate voice, making it impossible for anyone to be left unmoved.

Totally engrossed in the persona that he had created, he traveled far and wide sampling everything that this world had to offer. He left no town or city the same as he found it, as those he influenced tried to replicate whatever tour de force had a hold of him. But it may shock you which *force* he attributes to his success.

He spoke of a "spirit" who had convinced him to change his name in exchange for stardom. He said of himself, "I had forgotten all about God . . . Not knowing that I was directed and commanded by another power—the power of darkness, the power that you've heard so much about that a lot of people don't believe—the devil, Satan. We must realize that there is a force that is fighting against us in this world." And he knew all too well the scars that he bore from that struggle.

Though his family roots were Jewish, as a child, he had been brought up in a Pentecostal church, where his father was a preacher and he himself sang in the choir. But when Little Richard got a taste for showmanship, feeding upon the adulation that he received as a rising star, his appetite became insatiable. Several times over the years, he tried to escape the slavish lifestyle of self-exploitation that was harming his very soul and to seek after God, even to serve Jesus. But he was fettered by an invisible chain that, no matter how hard he tried, he could not free himself from.

Then, beyond his own strength and ability, he experienced one more transformation; but this time, it was truly radical. Little Richard said, "I gave up rock-and-roll for the Rock of Ages. I cut off my crown of hair for a crown of life." Why? What happened?

Rock Bottom

As a younger performer, Little Richard had been completely against drinking and drugs, even smoking regular cigarettes. In fact, he would fine members of his band who did get involved in such things. But steadily, as the pressures and expectations of the music industry weighed heavily upon him, he became enmeshed—hook, line, and sinker—by the very same. At a time when a typical man of color would earn around $10 a day, Little Richard was sometimes spending over a $1000 a day on his self-destructive habits.

His struggle was not just with substance abuse; he was also obsessed by a promiscuous life of sexual fascination. Many times, he bore testimony to how his shameful behavior degraded both himself and others. And though the bad company he kept was leading him further and further astray, it was only when he accepted that it was actually the devil who was controlling his mind, enslaving him to lust and a self-harming lifestyle, that he begged Jesus to set him free.

Mercifully, during that time, God used various terrifying and tragic events to wake him up to the reality of eternity. On one occasion, a friend turned up at his house with a gun and was determined to kill him because he owed him money. Although they were close, Little Richard knew the person was high on drugs and, therefore, not in full control of himself.

Little Richard's birthday was on December 5; and one year, he went to another friend's house to celebrate it by picking up a package of cocaine. But what frightened him were the few and foreboding words that particular friend uttered as he handed over the package: "Take care of yourself, old man."

Little Richard remembers, "I didn't realize . . . that he was gonna die that night. He wasn't sick, not unto death, but he died that night. That night, he died." This shocked Little Richard to the core. What if it had been him?

Such scenes twisted into the thinning fabric of his own downward-spiraling life, stained by drugs and debauchery, they led him to draw closer to God. During a recording, before a live audience, he declared his simple faith:

> Jesus loves you. What am I supposed to do without Jesus? I need Jesus in my life. You need Jesus in your life. You need to give up drugs and let Jesus have His way in your life. What the world needs today is Jesus, and to keep the Ten Commandments, and to read the Bible from Genesis to Revelation. What am I supposed to do without Jesus?[67]

Through a testimony like Little Richard's, we can see that God's grace is greater than our worst sin. Oh yes, he had made

---

[67] Some of Little Richard's testimony featured here also appears on his record, *God's Beautiful City* (Black Label Records, 1982).

mistakes—huge mistakes! Again and again! But God wouldn't let him go. Mercifully, He kept bringing him back to the fold.

You may not have sunk to such depths of depravity. But sin is sin, and every sin is a greater offense to a holy God than we can ever imagine. Praise God that there is full and free forgiveness for each one of us—no matter how far we have strayed or for how long—if only we humble ourselves, look to Jesus, and plead for mercy.

From Performer to Preacher

Now, Little Richard became ever more preoccupied with preaching than performing. He would constantly hand out Christian leaflets, booklets, and Bibles freely to fans. He would take every opportunity to witness about the love of Jesus to his fellow celebrities. And was always looking for opportunities to use his media platform to draw attention to how God had changed his life and that Jesus was his only Hope.

On the *Late Show With David Letterman* in 1982, he announced that he had been delivered by God from a homosexual lifestyle and was now committing his time to be a traveling evangelist. David Letterman didn't quite know what to make of it all and quickly changed the subject.

From what Little Richard said in many interviews, it is clear that he would want to be remembered more as a prodigal son who was welcomed back time and time again into the Father's house (Luke 15:11-32) than for his time as a rebel rocker.

It's true that many times in his life, he struggled to walk closely with his Lord. There are certainly numerous distractions in the music industry. And so often the "friends" of celebrities are more concerned with milking the cash cow than showing any real concern for the spiritual state of the one they claim to care about. They will do anything and say anything to keep their golden goose idol from any truly Christian influence. And as so much travel is typically involved, it's hard to settle into a church and come under good teaching and the pastoral care that they need so much. Yet Little Richard knew how important it was to have a transformed life, which is proof that someone's faith in Jesus is real and that God is at work in them. This is why he highlighted the necessity of the Ten Commandments (God's moral code) and reading the Bible to better know the God Who rescues us from ourselves.

For if there is no desire to live in a way that is pleasing to God, nor to grow in grace and to better know Him Who lovingly foreknew us, then it is possible we are self-deceived. Such a person is still in need of saving from their own deceptive heart, from the dominion of sin in their lives, and from the wrath of a holy God under Whose condemnation we all are in our natural fallen state. Praise God for His mercy.

Another Prodigal Son

Now, let's travel to another century and to another continent to someone no one would put in the same book, let alone the same chapter as Little Richard. But after all is said and *sung*, we will discover that they were not so different. Who might this be? See if you can guess:

This soul survivor confesses, "The frenzy [for sex] gripped me and I surrendered myself entirely to lust."[68] This person went on to live

---

68 St. Augustine, "The Brambles of Lust," Lapham's Quarterly, Accessed November 10, 2024, https://www.laphamsquarterly.org/eros/brambles-lust.

for a decade with a woman who was not his wife, fathering a child with her more out of carelessness than love. He refused to marry her; and eventually, she left him. He put it down to the fact that "she was stronger than I." He wasn't opposed to marriage; he tried to marry a young girl two years below the legal age. But as the wait became unbearable, "impatient of the delay," and "a slave to lust," he soon found himself in the embrace of yet another. The only constant in his depraved life was his thoughtlessness toward his mother's broken heart, as she wept and prayed for him daily.

What this young man did with his body was the wretched outworking of a calloused heart in rebellion against God. His mind had been poisoned and confused for some time by a cult whose heretical teaching was very popular in his day. It took a sprinkling of biblical truths and scraps of other religions, then twisted and wove them to create new meanings and a religion which spanned from the Roman Empire to China, from the third to fourteenth century. The cult religion was called Manichaeism.[69]

This unlikely lad eventually became the bishop of Hippo in North Africa in the fourth century. His name was Augustine of Hippo. History records—and few theologians, whatever their persuasion, would disagree—he was the most influential mind in Christianity in the last fifteen hundred years! He helped many Christians in his day to reform their Christian faith according to biblical truth. He did this through his copious writings and debates, which include a thirteen-volume set

---

69   Manichaeism was a type of gnosticism (gnosis—of spiritual truth). This religion was very complex and dealt with a battle between light and darkness, in which humans are the unfortunate victims who participate in different degrees. In this religion, the spiritual is basically good, while that which is material is evil. Mani, the cult's founder from Iran, claimed to be a prophet who carried God's latest revelation necessary for unity, peace, and salvation for its adherents.

called *Confessions*, which is really the first ever Christian autobiography: giving many insights into his heart and mind pre- and post-salvation.[70]

From Playboy to Preacher

What straightened out this careless rebel? What compelled his depraved mind to step out of the darkness and into the light, from depression to joyful fellowship with the One Who is *"the* way and *the* truth and *the* life" (John 14:6, italics mine)—Whose name is Jesus?

Every other *way* had led him into perversion externally and desperation internally. Every other *truth* had, in essence, been a lie in fancy dress that had deceived him. And he could never have truly enjoyed *life*—not the fullness thereof—until he learned to put his faith in Christ alone (John 10:10).

Some would attribute the epic change in the man—from sinner to saint, from playboy to preacher—to the prayers of his long-suffering mother, Monica. She had prayed, and the Lord had heard. God uses such means; it's true. But both Augustine and his mother would agree that the soul-saving work was due to God's amazing grace—also known as *saving* grace![71] [72]

While still lost in the world Augustine had concluded that his sins were too great, that he had waited too long, and that he had

---

70   His soteriology (doctrine of salvation) helped define the Protestant church's understanding more than any other post biblical hero of the faith. His ecclesiology (doctrine of church government and practice) helped shape the Roman Catholic church more than any other "church father," a title given to the most influential Christian thinkers from the first five centuries of Church history.
71   See Appendix B.
72   Romans 11:6, 1 Corinthians 15:10, 2 Timothy 2:1, 2 Peter 1:2, 2 Peter 3:18, Revelation 22:21.

wasted too much time for there to be any hope for him. One of his problems was that he had a love/hate relationship with his sin. "[My] real pleasure consisted in doing something that was forbidden. The evil in me was foul, but I loved it."[73] But when God began to move upon his soul, everything changed.

First came the realization that something was profoundly wrong inside of him, something that neither he nor anyone else could resolve. His great escapades in life had actually been expressions of the fact that he was spiritually dead. His constant lack of peace confirmed that he not only feared physical death but also the wrath of God, the judgment he would face on the final day—a thought from which he had been trying to distract himself. This now bore down upon him as a crushing weight.

Then, unexpectedly, a Divine light penetrated his darkness! Augustine confessed:

> I was speaking and weeping in the most bitter contrition of my heart, when, lo! I heard from a neighboring house a voice, as of a boy or girl, I know not, chanting, and oft repeating, "Take up and read; Take up and read." Instantly, my countenance altered . . . I arose; interpreting it to be no other than a command from God to open the Book and read the first chapter I should find . . . I seized, opened, and in silence read that section on which my eyes first fell: "Not in rioting and drunkenness, not in chambering and wantonness, not in strife and envying; but put ye on the Lord Jesus Christ, and make not provision for the flesh" . . . Instantly at the end of this

---

73 "Augustine of Hippo," Christianity Today online, August 8, 2008, https://www.christianitytoday.com/2008/08/augustine-of-hippo.

sentence, by a light . . . infused into my heart, all the darkness of doubt vanished away.[74]

In a prayer, he later concluded, "For there exists a delight that is not given to the wicked, but to those honoring Thee, O God, without desiring recompense, the joy of whom Thou art Thyself! And this is the blessed life, to rejoice towards Thee, about Thee, for Thy sake . . . Thou hast made us for thyself, O Lord, and our heart is restless until it finds its rest in thee."[75]

Finally, after years of deprivation and distress, Augustine had found rest. He discovered that there was true and lasting peace through faith in Jesus Christ—as Savior, to be trusted and as Lord, to be served. But this newfound *rest* certainly did not involve inactivity. His writing was prolific, taking the form of sermons, lectures, and letters, many of which survive today. Augustine believed that "God has promised forgiveness to your repentance, but He has not promised tomorrow to your procrastination."[76]

Oh yes, we are saved to serve, which we will explore in a later chapter. But what of this amazing saving grace? Augustine went on to say, "In my deepest wound I saw your glory, and it dazzled me."[77] He also said, "I have read in Plato and Cicero sayings that are wise and very beautiful; but I have never read in either of them: 'Come unto

---

[74] Augustine of Hippo, Chapter 12, in *Confessions of Saint Augustine*, Vol. 9 (London: Penguin Books, 1961).
[75] Augustine. *Confessions*, trans. by Rex Warner (New York: Mentor, 1963).
[76] Augustine of Hippo, "Sermon 73A," *Sermons*, Vol.. III (Brooklyn: New City Press, 1991), 296.
[77] Augustine of Hippo, quoted in Fr. Joseph Mary Elder, "Stigmata of St. Francis: 3 Ways for Holiness," Capuchins, September 13, 2017, https://www.capuchins.org/posts/stigmata-of-st-francis-3-ways-for-holiness.

me all ye that labour and are heavy laden.'"[78] These words first came from the lips of Jesus Himself. But to whom is He calling?

Jesus Calls the Harassed and Helpless

He calls battered moralists, bruised legalists, and those who have come to the realization that their best could never be good enough. That *nearly* good enough is still bad. That *nearly* alive is still dead. That *nearly* there is still to have fallen short.

Oh, what medicine to the soul to hear Jesus say, "I will give you rest" (Matt. 11:28)—not mediated rest through a saint, Mary, or an angel: Jesus Himself gives rest to all who come to Him believing in Who He is and in What He has done for them. Augustine, as already considered from Little Richard's testimony, came to understand that "The law detects, [but] grace alone conquers sin"[79]—and this through faith in Jesus alone!

When Jesus was dying on the cross, after perfectly fulfilling all the requirements of the Law, He could say, "'It is finished!'" (John 19:30). He left nothing for you to do but believe upon what He had done in your place. "If you declare with your mouth, 'Jesus is Lord,'[80] and believe in your heart that God raised him from the dead, you will be saved. For it is with your heart that you believe and are

---

78 Carl Sundell, "The True St. Augustine," Catholic Insight online, August 28, 2023, https://catholicinsight.com/the-true-saint-augustine.
79 Augustine of Hippo, quoted in John Sartelle, "Grace-Based Ethics," *Table Talk* online, August 29, 2010, https://www.ligonier.org/learn/devotionals/grace-based-ethics?srsltid=AfmBOooBSNrSlRR2TvzsioBksPxQ_af3j5v0gR-pO5ohMMt3wLdfoZlu.
80 In Greek, Lord—"kuros"— is commonly used to simply mean "sir/master." But when used in relation to Jesus, it points people to the Hebrew equivalent, "Adonai," the spoken form of YHWH. These are Divine titles! To claim that "Jesus is Lord" is to recognize that He is God incarnate in the flesh.

justified, and it is with your mouth that you profess your faith and are saved" (Rom. 10:9-10).

"Justified" means that you are considered right with God—*just* before Him, "*just*-as-if-you-had-never-sinned"—and as if we had kept the whole Law of God, which Jesus did on our behalf. That's why Romans 8:1, 33-34 says, "Therefore, there is *now* no condemnation for those who are in Christ Jesus . . . Who will bring any charge against those whom God has chosen? It is God who justifies. Who then is the one who condemns? No one. Christ Jesus who died—more than that, who was raised to life—is at the right hand of God and is also interceding for us."

Those who believe are saved by Christ's finished redemptive work here on earth and are kept by His ongoing intercessory work there in Heaven. Read the whole chapter of Romans 8 to better appreciate these verses. Also, Hebrews 7:25 says, "He is able to save *completely* those who come to God through him, because he always lives to intercede for them."

The true profession of the Christian is not with words only; anyone can say the words, "Jesus is Lord," but only those who *believe* in their hearts will be saved. This is where God graciously does His work. Augustine understood this only too well. "Nothing whatever pertaining to godliness and real holiness can be accomplished without grace."[81] He said, "Give me the grace [O Lord] to do as You command, and command me to do what You will . . . O holy God . . . when Your commands are obeyed, it is from You that we receive the

---

81 Augustine of Hippo, quoted in Peter Amsterdam, "More Like Jesus: Reflections on Faithfulness and Holiness," *Directors' Corner*, The Family International, June 16, 2020, https://directors.tfionline.com/post/more-jesus-reflections-faithfulness-and-holiness/.

power to obey them."[82] No one can speak these words with conviction if the Spirit has not begun a work in their heart.

Why Was Christ's Resurrection Essential?

It is necessary to believe in Christ's resurrection from the dead because that was how Christ Jesus proved His victory over death, sin, and Satan. Death could not hold Him in the grave. "The wages of sin is death" (Rom. 6:23). Christ had paid the price in full! Satan is already defeated and knows it. That is why "'he is filled with fury, because he knows that his time is short'" (Rev. 12:12b). But we need not fear him. In fact, he fears those who are in communion with the Savior. "Submit yourselves, then, to God. Resist the devil, and he will flee from you" (James 4:7).

Eternal salvation cannot be earned or merited by anything we have done, can do, or will do in the future. There is nothing even mildly good in us that drew God's attention to us as the cause of His pity, the reason for His love. We deserve only His wrath and subsequent punishment. We have all done our version of Little Richard's and Augustine of Hippo's perversions. We have all been rebels and God-haters, even if we don't realize the depths to which we have sunk. Everything we receive from our faithful Creator less than death is mercy! And if He condescends to hear your prayers and to save your soul, that is nothing short of His *amazing grace*.

What a difference this grace made in Augustine's life! One thousand years after he was promoted to glory, God used his writings to spark the

---

82 Augustine of Hippo, quoted in John Piper, "For Men: Augustine, Sin, and Sovereign Joy" (lecture, the Campus Outreach National Conference, Chattanooga, Tennessee, December 31, 2011).

Reformation,[83] which had as its motto, "After darkness, light." As darkness was the inevitable result of cold, stillborn legalism, so light floods into the soul as the faithful are inspired to return to the Word of God—the only spiritual authority God has given to be the rule for our lives.

Augustine had been rescued, and like a spiritual lark, he could sing to God in prayer:

> How sweet all at once it was for me to be rid of those fruitless joys which I had once feared to lose . . . You drove them from me, you who are the true, the sovereign joy. You drove them from me and took their place, you who are sweeter than all pleasure . . . you who outshine all light, yet are hidden deeper than any secret in our hearts, you who surpass all honor . . . O Lord my God, my Light, my Wealth, and my Salvation.[84]

You are saved by *grace* alone, in *Christ* alone, through *faith* alone, according to the *Scriptures* alone and for the *glory of God* alone—or you are not saved! Do you share Augustine's sentiments as expressed in this prayer? "Oh, God, to know you is life. To serve You is freedom. To praise you is the soul's joy and delight. Guard me with the power of Your grace here and in all places. Now and at all times, forever. Amen."[85] I am sure Little Richard would add his own shrill and excited "AMEN!" to that.

---

83 The *Great* Reformation was the result of a *great* movement of the Spirit of God, who led the Church to re-examine its doctrines and practices according to the Scriptures alone.

84 St. Augustine, quoted in John Piper, *The Legacy of Sovereign Joy: God's Triumphant Grace in the Lives of Augustine, Luther, and Calvin*, Vol. 1 (Wheaton: Crossway, 2006), 40.

85 Augustine of Hippo, "Oh, God, to know you is life. To serve You . . . ," theysaidso.com, Accessed June 7, 2024 https://theysaidso.com/quote/augustine-of-hippo-oh-god-to-know-you-is-life-to-serve-you-is-freedom-to-praise.

CHAPTER 7
The God We Serve

What do you love most? Who do you value above all? Take a moment to think about that. In order to discover the character of people, we have only to observe what they love. Augustine said, "Christ is not valued at all, unless he is valued above all."[86]

Every culture in every age is decorated by their stories of love lost and found. These affect their literature, paintings, fashion, architecture, and, of course, music—a great majority of all popular songs in the West have a love theme. But what is *true* love? It's certainly not the stupefied, fairytale imposter that feeds on superficiality and is often drunk with sensuality. So, what is it? What does love in its purest form look like?

"This is love: not that we loved God, but that He loved us and sent His Son as an atoning sacrifice for our sins" (1 John 4:10). And this sacrificial act becomes even more profound when you realize that for all eternity Jesus has been the object of the Father's love (John 17:24), as affirmed at Jesus' baptism, where He said, "'This is my Son, whom I love; with Him I am well pleased'" (Matt. 3:17). Just three years later, this same Son would literally love us to His death on a Roman cross! What more could God have done to prove His love?

---

86 Augustine of Hippo, quoted in Paul Lee Tan, *Encyclopedia of 7,700 Illustrations* (Garland: Bible Communications, Inc., 1996).

God Channels His Love Through Us

And yet there is more. It pleases God to channel His love into the hearts of His people, that He might continue to put it on display through the lives of His adopted children. How does that work? As we serve one another,[87] consider others' needs before your own. Meditate on Philippians 2:1-4. This is easier said than done, a daily challenge for which we need much grace and a close walk with the Spirit of God.

This is an application of Jesus' words, "'A new command I give you: Love one another. As I have loved you, so you must love one another. By this everyone will know that you are my disciples, if you love one another'" (John 13:34-35). That's right—how we love each other confirms our discipleship and spiritual maturity. We must be motivated by God's unconditional and soul-saving love for us, which in turn will prompt us to ask Him for more empathy and courage to act upon the opportunities He gives us to show just how much we love *Him*.

The simplest definition of a Christian is someone who follows Christ. In ancient days, disciples of a rabbi followed their master wherever he went. When he stopped and sat down to teach, they stopped and sat down to listen. What he taught, they did. This principle carries over into Christianity, although our disciple/Master relationship with Christ goes much deeper. Christianity is not just something we *do*; it characterizes what we *are*. "See what great love the Father has lavished on us, that we should be called children of God! And that is what we are!" (1 John 3:1).

---

[87] There are around sixty "one another" and "each other" passages in the New Testament. I suggest reading and praying through them, asking God to help you live them out among His people.

United with God

Over 180 in the New Testament, the phrase "in Christ," and its equivalent including "Christ in them/us," is affirmed, which agrees with what Peter tells us when he said that we "participate in the divine nature" (2 Peter 1:4). But what does that mean? We become little gods? That's the error of Mormonism and some prosperity teachers. No, it means that the only true God restores His image in us when we come to faith in Who Jesus is and in what was accomplished by His life and death.

Unlike inanimate objects and animals that have no self-awareness or even unlike angels, despite being "ministering spirits" (Heb. 1:14), God has made man to be *like* Him (Gen. 1:26-28). From this, we derive our mutual human dignity, self-awareness, and sense of rationality, morality, and ethical understanding. This makes us responsible creatures and sufficiently endowed to rule over God's creation as His co-regents, subduing the world through cultivation to make it ever more productive, even as we are being fruitful and filling it, just as He commissioned our first parents, Adam and Eve.

We are also like God when we express "love, joy, peace, forbearance, kindness, goodness, faithfulness, gentleness and self-control" (Gal. 5:22-23), although, tragically, our original desire and ability to practice the above with true motives to image God were corrupted and incapacitated by the Fall. Instead, we inherit a "sinful nature" much more prone to "sexual immorality, impurity and debauchery; idolatry and witchcraft; hatred, discord, jealousy, fits of rage, selfish ambition, dissensions, factions and envy; drunkenness, orgies, and the like" (Gal. 5:19-21).

Then just when all seems permanently lost and hopeless, now, with the wonder of salvation, this same desire and ability to live in accordance with God's will are restored to us as His Spirit abides in us. We are still a work in progress, being sanctified, and fail Him daily. But as Christians, we have now re-entered into fellowship with our faithful Creator as adopted children in a pure love relationship with our Heavenly Father through His eternal Son, our Lord and Savior, by the internal working of the Holy Spirit (1 John. 1:3, Rom. 8:5-17). This is why everything that Christians are called to do, we should do willingly as an expression of our love for God.

The whole book of 1 John is given to us that we may better understand this fellowship with God and the fruit of love, truth, and good works which will flow from that. It is a great book to test our own hearts to see if we *really* are Christ's disciples, graciously saved and living by the Spirit.

The Fellowship of Believers

An example of how we express love for God is when we gather to worship with other likeminded Christians as a local church to pray, read and study the Bible, sing God's praises, and, as already stated, serve one another (Heb. 10:22-25; Eph. 5:19-21).

Additionally, as announced by Jesus shortly before returning to glory, we have the Great Commission to "go and make disciples of all nations . . . teaching them to obey everything I have commanded you" (Matt. 28:18-20). Surely our obedience to this command will take us outside of any cozy church building to where people are. This is so that others may also know the reality of God's Divine love, transcendent peace, and the pure joy that is ours as we commune with Him by His Spirit.

Nothing in the above list of Christian activities should be absent from our regular experience or should be considered burdensome. It's not for us to pick and choose what we will or will not do, prioritizing our personal comfort zone over God's will and pleasure. They ought to be the outworking of our Christian love and characterize the *ordinary* Christian life. In this, there is duty, labor, and very great reward (Luke 17:10; 1 Thess. 1:3; Rev. 22:12).

Now, let's put all this into a practical context, one that is another world to most people. And yet this will demonstrate that no matter who or where you are, these Christian activities should be practiced in *every* local church by *every* disciple of Christ.

Primal Christianity

Deep in the Brazilian rainforest—twenty hours by boat away from any road, shop, hospital or anything else that we might call *civilization*—is a small tribe of Apurinã Indians with whom I served as a missionary/pastor.

Oscar, a muscular and peaceable fisherman I was training for the preaching ministry, would often invite me to hunt with him. I would take a number of food supplies, water, spare clothing, and even some books all stuffed into a large backpack, then clamber in my boots behind him across logs and wade in swamps as we hacked our way through virgin forest, which resisted us at every step. Oscar, however, normally hunted barefooted with nothing but a rifle and a machete.

When we caught something, he would cut a strip of bark from a tree to make a sling to carry the meal home, although it was not uncommon after a six-hour trek for us to return to the little village with nothing. This was embarrassing. On such occasions, we would try to slink into our respective huts before anyone noticed. This was in contrast to when we did catch something. Then we would walk slowly through the center of the community with our tasty trophy strapped to our backs, retelling the heroic adventure to everyone we met.

It is fascinating how my Indian friends normally hunt with their ears and learn with their eyes. That's why the wilds of the Brazilian rainforest make for an excellent classroom, with numerous natural illustrations all around us.

On one hunting trip, after rowing our canoe through a number of creeks and walking for hours, I thought it would be a good idea to teach Oscar how to set some traps I had learned about on the internet. I hoped that they would increase our success rate.

The traps included a camouflaged platform, upon which a fruit-bait is carefully placed within a noose that has a trigger attached to a suspended log. But after several days, the critters continually outwitted us, and we had little success. But it wasn't a waste of time. It was an opportunity for discipleship training, for which I was more experienced than trapping. I was able to teach about the need for perseverance and to be mindful of our total dependence upon God in order that we might be even more effective and productive in His service.

On that occasion, as we passed a muddy water-hole, I was also able to impress upon Oscar the essential place of preaching in the life of the church to feed God's people. I told him, "As with a water hole that animals come to drink from, if it dries up, they will go elsewhere to be refreshed or simply die. Similarly, the Bible is our source of nourishment. The people must be watered and fed from it regularly. If there is no preaching or the preaching is bad, then the true people of God will go elsewhere to be fed or suffer malnourishment and become weak in their faith" (2 Tim. 2:14-26; 1 Cor. 2:1-5).

We finally returned to his open-sided, stilted, and thatched hut with two monkeys to skin for tea. And there was his young wife, Ana-lúcia, sitting cross-legged on the floor with four of her children, reading to them from the Bible in her mother tongue. With her waist-long, jet-black, shiny hair cascading over her shoulders and her round face beaming, she looked quite angelic. I knew of her faithfulness in leading the ladies' Bible study group for years, even during times when the church had closed down on a number of occasions; but I wanted to know how she had become a Christian.

She responded very simply, "When I was a girl, the missionaries explained about Jesus in the Bible,[88] and some of the people who were my parents' age became Christians. So, I read the Bible all the way through but felt nothing. Then I prayed and asked God to help me understand it. I read it through again. Then I believed."

I was eager to know, "What did you believe?"

She responded with refreshing clarity, "That Jesus said He came to save me. I trusted Him. I knew it was true."

The Apurinã use few words to communicate—in Portuguese, that is. They do, however, seem to use many more sounds at double speed in their own language. They also have a curious habit of letting their sentences trail off into a mumble once they think that

---

88 When the Apurinã refer to the Bible, they usually mean the New Testament, as this is almost all they have in their language. Admittedly, they do have Genesis, Exodus, and fifty-one Psalms; but these are seldom read and even less understood by most for lack of good, consistent teaching.

you understand their general point. Ana-lúcia is quite typical of the Christians in the tribe, who really do have a childlike and beautiful faith. They conclude that if the Bible says it, then it must be true (Matt. 18:1-4; 2 Tim. 3:16-17). Certainly, her life bears a wonderful witness to the honesty of her testimony.

Interestingly her Bible knowledge and ability to read far exceed that of her husband, Oscar, who is already responsible for preaching, so she humbly helps him in the preparation of his messages and prays for him earnestly.

There is no doubt that her spiritual maturity is a gift, one which she has used to care for the spiritual welfare of the other Christian ladies in the tribe since her conversion fifteen years earlier.

Many times over the years, church services in the once wooden and thatched church building, now stone and aluminum, would only sporadically take place. It was common for months to pass without anyone to visit and to preach a sermon. But without fail, Ana-Lúcia, in her calm, loving, and bright way, continued to meet with the ladies, rain or shine, day or night, to teach them God's words.

In and Out of Season

Attending services rain or shine, day or night should not be passed over too quickly. When it rains, the torrents fall from the sky as if you were standing under a waterfall. The noise upon the aluminum roof is deafening! Outside, the rain bounces up from the ground to waist height and strips the paint off walls in just one season. Then, when the sun shines, the temperatures can reach forty degrees Celsius with one hundred percent humidity and no breeze.

There would often be a puddle of sweat around my Bible where my arms rested on the desk as I studied.

Many come to the services by canoe, weaving through a sunken forest. All have to walk, most barefooted across thorny ground in the dry season. Whether paddling or hiking, you can feel your energy sapping every second.

Once inside the church building, the temperature can become almost unbearable; people constantly shuffle their chairs around to avoid the direct sunlight, which beams in through giant open shutters. Then at night, while outside is pitch black with many a concealed danger, inside, it becomes a feeding frenzy for ankle-biting mosquitoes, making the most of the shadows that the wheezing generator is unable to illuminate.

If you were to ask Ana-Lúcia, "Considering these challenges, why even bother going to church?" she would likely answer you by quoting the name written above the door of their church building, which alludes to their denomination of just one local fellowship, translated as, "Where God meets with His people." She knows that God is present everywhere. But she also knows that God blesses His people as they gather together in His Name to worship Him to be fed by the Spirit of God through the faithful preaching of His Word.

Love God? Then Love His People

If you love God, you will love His people. If you love being with God, then you will love being with His people. In fact, I would go so far as to say that you only truly love God to the degree that you love His people. And being part of a local church fellowship is the context in which we can demonstrate this love as we worship Him and serve alongside each other.

Which Day Did God Set Apart as Holy?

Does a local church have to gather on Sundays to be considered part of the universal Church? Isn't the Sabbath supposed to be a Saturday, the day some Jews still maintain as holy?

The word *sabbath* refers to a principle more than a specific day of the week. The principle is a seven-day cycle that, in regard to God's people, begins with a day of rest from worldly labors, which is our blessing—a day made holy, set a part by the Lord for worship (Gen. 2:2-3). God says to His people that it is "a sign between me and you for the generations to come, so you may know that I am the LORD, who makes you holy" (Exod. 31:13). It is a holy day for a holy people to worship a holy God (Exod. 20:8).

During the five years I regularly visited the Apurinã, I taught them that although we have our roots in Old Testament Judaism, the Church blossoms in New Testament Christianity. True believers from both ages are those who trust in God to provide salvation through Christ Jesus. Those living prior to His revelation lived by faith, anticipating His arrival (Job 19:25-27; Hab. 1-3). Those living since He has come until the end of time live by faith also, believing in the success of His salvific ministry. There is ultimately one Church, made up of Jew and Gentile, one true Israel, one holy nation saved by the one Savior, Jesus (1 Peter 2:9; Eph. 2:11-22; Gal. 3:26-29).

When Jesus fulfilled the Law (Matt. 5:17-18), He fulfilled the whole sacrificial system that had been in place for fifteen hundred years

(Heb. 10). Now, there needed to be a distinction between those who rejected Jesus as the Messiah and continued in Judaism and those who believed and were dedicated to follow Him, eventually being called Christians (Acts 11:26).

Very soon, Christians began meeting on Sundays, the first day of the week (Acts 20:7; 1 Cor. 16:2). They did this because Jesus was raised from the dead on a Sunday (John 20:19); thus, it was called "the Lord's Day" (Rev. 1:10). The Holy Spirit also descended upon the early church in Acts 2 on a Sunday.[89] All through the centuries, on every continent, the New Testament Church has gathered together for corporate worship on Sundays, which has become a powerful witness to the world.

And yet, strictly speaking, we should be worshipping God *every* day, wherever we are and with whomever (Psalm 1:1-2; 1 Thess. 5:16-18; Eph. 5:15-20). We are taught that the first Christians met together *every* day for worship, formally and informally (Acts 2:42-47).

Whether services take place in purpose-built/bought buildings or someone's home really doesn't matter. The place of worship needs to be a practical size, matching the size and needs of the fellowship meeting there.

Biblical Leadership

But what is essential is that there is a recognized leadership responsible for teaching and caring for the members, both spiritually and practically. The primary responsibility of elders (also called

---

89 This happened on the day that was also called "Pentecost," celebrated fifty days after the Passover. You can learn more about its history in Leviticus 23 and see its significance fulfilled in Acts 2.

pastors/shepherds)[90] is to oversee the spiritual welfare of Christ's flock, the Church. Their qualifications are found in 1 Timothy 3:1-7 and Titus 1:6-9. Although the elders are responsible for every aspect of church life, they may delegate certain responsibilities which might otherwise keep them from their primary focus of prayer and preaching (Acts 6:2-4).

Deacon is the second office that God has ordained to care for His Church. The title simply means "servant." Their qualifications, found in 1 Timothy 3:8-13, are very similar to that of elder but without the necessity of being gifted to teach. Their practical service to the local body of believers can be varied and oftentimes nondescript. Often, the more faithfully they serve, the more their service goes unnoticed and the more they are taken for granted. This can be true even of deacons who serve in the jungle, where one of their responsibilities is to check the building for tarantulas and to dispose of them. Another is to keep the grass short around the building with a machete and to douse ants' nests with petrol, then set fire to them. And yet another is rowing or literally carrying the elderly and infirm to and from church.

Together, elders and deacons will be involved in the church organization and discipline that all things will be done orderly and every member cared for and given opportunity to participate in the worship of God through obedient service to Jesus (1 Peter 1:2).

---

90   *Elders* are also referred to as "overseers," "bishops," and "pastors." These four titles are synonymous and refer to the same office, although highlight different aspects of the person's responsibility. There is no biblical teaching to suggest a hierarchy or distinction between those who bear these titles.

Universal Principles

The reason why I am using the church of the Apurinã in the Brazilian rainforest to illustrate this chapter is really to draw attention to the universal principles and simplicity of ecclesiology (the study of the church). Wherever the Church of Jesus Christ is, it belongs to Him; He purchased it with His blood, and He is building it (Matt. 16:18).

The Church is not an institution to serve man but "a chosen people, a royal priesthood, a holy nation, God's special possession" to worship God and to proclaim His Gospel (1 Peter 2:9). It is certainly not a business and operates on totally different principles—not to make a profit, but to invest money in Christ's service. The Church is a family within a spiritual Kingdom. We are adopted brothers and sisters with the same Heavenly Father serving the same King Jesus.

"Doing Church"

Interestingly, Jesus' commission to the church at the end of Matthew's gospel[91] presupposes evangelism as the natural activity for every believer. Surely, this is the purpose for each one of us remaining here on earth; after being saved, we may bear witness to the necessity and sufficiency of Christ Jesus as both Lord and Savior. Even as together we "[teach] them to obey everything" that Christ has "commanded" us to believe and to practice (Matt. 28:20). This is why it is so strange that many churches today do not teach well that every

---

91 Variations of the Great Commission can be found toward the end of each of the four gospels and toward the beginning of the book of Acts (Matt. 28:18-20; Mark 15:16; Luke 24:46-47; John 20:21-23; Acts 1:8).

member of the church is to "make disciples" (Matt. 28:19), as every one of us is to be involved in the Great Commission.

Wonderfully, deep in the Amazonian jungle lands, the Apurinã not only understand this but are also unreservedly practicing all of the above, as they seek to be faithful to the Lord's instructions. This is why they recognize the only two sacraments that make up the one ordinance given to us by the Lord Jesus—believer's baptism,[92] to bear witness to our entrance into the family of God and the Lord's Supper, to remind us of our life in Christ with the bread and wine representing His broken body and shed blood offered on our behalf to secure our salvation (1 Cor. 11:17-34). Whereas believers are baptized just once, we remember the Lord's death regularly until He comes back to earth. For some churches, this means weekly, for others monthly, for some annually. For a period of five years, I visited the Indians every two months for three-week visits. The Lord's Supper was always the first service that we enjoyed together. We would dedicate the whole Sunday morning to it, with bread that I had freshly baked and wine that was made from a local fruit.

Heartfelt Singing

The Apurinã have around one hundred hymns and songs they frequently sing in worship in their own language. Though most

---

[92] Believers baptism is taught by Jesus (Matt. 28:19) and the apostles (Acts 2:38-41). The person is briefly immersed in water, used as a visible outward sign of spiritual renewal and cleanliness, accompanied by a "pledge of a good conscience toward God" (1 Peter 3:21) to proclaim the invisible inward work of the Holy Spirit, who has applied the finished redemptive work of Christ to the believer.

are translated from well-known British and American hymns from the nineteenth and twentieth centuries, some are popular modern hymns and a few even composed by their own people. The Apurinã leadership agree that we are wise to have a balance of what they consider to be the best of the old with the best of the new. This way, they hope to avoid only singing classics which some struggle to understand, and from disappearing into a hyper-emotional, man-centered, narcissistic pity party and risk forsaking their biblical roots, carried along by any new "wind of teaching" (Eph. 4:14).

Our Spiritual Lifeline

Lastly, there is one hugely important and central element in the life of the believer, necessary for the health of the whole family of God, reserved until now—prayer. I would meet with the Apurinã leaders each weekday morning for discipleship and leadership training and always begin in prayer. Then, after a couple of hours, I would ask one of them to close our time in prayer. This is also what we would do in each of our public services. But maybe because of the language barrier or because I didn't live permanently among them or because of an oversight on my own behalf, they had no actual prayer meeting! In fact, for the past ten years, without any ordained pastors, they had never had a regular corporate prayer meeting! Once God brought this to our attention, we knew something had to be done.

At the very next Sunday evening service, the church leaders announced, "If you are a Christian, then come to a special meeting of prayer on Tuesday." So they did. We had put out just a few chairs, like you might for such a meeting in the U.K with such short notice. But as *every* Christian came, the circle steadily grew and grew, until a second circle had to be put outside of that one even after the service had begun!

We began by focusing our minds and prayers with a Psalm, accompanied by a short commentary that I had written for each one. Then we went around the circle asking for prayer requests. Everyone, young and old, had a request without fail. Then I explained how as adopted children of grace we have the very great privilege of having a heart-to-heart with our Heavenly Father. So, one by one, everyone prayed! All fifty people present prayed without exception! It was one of the purest and most heavenly prayer meetings of which I have ever been blessed to be a part.

It struck me afresh what a gift prayer is. It is truly our lifeline with our Heavenly Father—a means by which we may bear each other's burdens and joys to Him Who cares for us (1 Peter 5:7). We can't change His will through prayer, but He changes us and condescends to actualize His Sovereign purposes through our prayers—an experience we are blessed to enjoy together, as well as alone. We can pray anytime, anywhere, out loud or in silence, with long prayers or short ones, just spending time in the presence of the Spirit of God. Oh, Lord, help us never neglect such a gift.

We began this chapter with some thoughts from Augustine of Hippo. Let's close it with an excerpt from one of his prayers. "Breathe in me, O Holy Spirit, that my thoughts may all be holy. Act in me, O Holy Spirit, that my work, too, may be holy. Draw my heart, O Holy

Spirit, that I love but what is holy. Strengthen me, O Holy Spirit, to defend all that is holy. Guard me, then, O Holy Spirit, that I always may be holy."[93]

---

[93] Augustine of Hippo, quoted in Antipas L. Harris, *Holy Living: Toward A Practical Theology* (Eugene: Wipf and Stock, 2013).

CHAPTER 8
The God Who Saves for His Glory

Who wants to live forever? Some people can't handle a question like that. It makes them feel uncomfortable. In 1986, the rock band Queen posed the question as a title for a song that highlighted the dilemma of an immortal warrior and his mortal love interest in the film, *The Highlander* (1986). The song, as with the film, is melancholic and implies that *forever* is basically just a lot of time that would inevitably become an unbearable tragedy without end.

So, why do people try so hard to prolong their life by avoiding death, whatever the cost? Cynically, we might conclude that the point of entertainment is to distract us from thinking about the inevitable question: What's next? Where might we land after we "shuffle off this mortal coil?"

Now, brace yourself. Where are *you* going to spend eternity?

Annihilation Is Not an Option

Imagine walking along a corridor with no windows and only two doors—a closed one behind you and an open one before you through which blinding light is leaping in every direction. Your heart is racing, even though you are dead. Yes, you just died—how, when, and where doesn't matter now. You are about to face your Creator God. Why should He let you into Heaven?

Some unbelievers try to draw some cold comfort from the idea of annihilation—that immediately, or shortly, after death, we cease to exist. Jesus says, "'They [referring to the wicked] will go away to *eternal* punishment, but the righteous to *eternal* life'" (Matt. 25:46, italics mine). Annihilation is not an option.

No one from reading the Bible could conclude that eternal life for the righteous actually just means a long period of time that will sooner or later end in annihilation. It speaks of a never-ending state of being, enjoying a blissful quality of that existence with Christ forever!

Now we must be consistent, as the same Greek word translated as *eternal*, referring to *life*, is the very same word connected to the punishment of the wicked. Either they both have a termination date, or they are both never-ending. And yes, as touched upon in chapter five, Hell is a real place created by God (Matt. 25:41), where all without saving faith in Jesus go, regardless of one's age or cultural background or opportunity to hear the Gospel. Surely, this is a very sobering thought for everyone.

The natural state of someone without faith in Jesus is abhorrent to God. The theological term is "total depravity."[94] It is only through hearing and responding humbly to the Gospel that someone can be saved. "Consequently, faith comes from hearing the message, and the message is heard through the word about Christ" (Rom. 10:17). It is

---

94 Genesis 6:5, 8:21; Psalm 51:5; Ecclesiastes 9:3; Isaiah 64:6; Jeremiah 17:9; 1 Corinthians 2:14; Ephesians 2:1-3; Romans 3:23.

easy to overlook the central significance of that passage in Romans. The apostle Paul is speaking of his great love for his own people, the Jews, who remained unsaved, despite receiving so many privileges, not the least of which was the Law of God which points consistently to Christ (Gal. 4:24). Although they had heard the message, the Gospel of Christ, they had not heard Christ calling them through that message while the preacher preached, "How can they believe in the one of whom they have not heard?" (Rom. 10:14). In the previous verse, Paul quoted Joel 2:32: "'Everyone who calls on the name of the LORD will be saved.'" In that verse, Joel goes on to say, "Whom the LORD calls." God must first call us before we can ever call upon Him; and He effectually calls all His blood-bought people through the proclamation of the Gospel (Rom. 10:20; John 10:16,26-27; Eph. 2:17; 1 Peter 1:10-12; 1 Cor. 2:9-16).

The Myth of Purgatory

Purgatory isn't an option either (as briefly discussed in chapter five). The idea is that after death and before being admitted into Heaven, there is a halfway-Hell-house where people receive punitive torture to *purge* them from their sin. It is a doctrine that was neither taught nor believed by anyone anywhere before the twelfth century, and there is certainly no passage in the Bible which teaches it.

Consider the apostle Paul's confidence to die in Philippians 1:20-24 and 2 Corinthians 5:1-10—neither of which speak about an intermediate state. This is a confidence that can be shared even by new converts, saved from a wicked background, having done nothing to earn any favor with God. This is illustrated by Jesus when

He assured the repentant, dying thief on a cross to His side, "'Truly I tell you, today you will be with me in paradise'" (Luke 23:43).

So the idea that in purgatory people's punishment is a necessary contribution toward their salvation undermines Christ's finished redemptive work upon the cross. Therefore, that doctrine is heretical. For otherwise, we would become co-redeemers with Christ and could demand that His glory be divided up for our services rendered.

"People Are Destined to Die Once, and After That to Face Judgment" (Heb. 9:27)

Therefore, this negates reincarnation as an option, despite the idea being around for about three thousand years, one thousand years before Christ. It features heavily in Hinduism, Buddhism, and Sikhism, as well as various veins of spiritism and New Ageism. The idea is that the better you do in this life, the more you will enjoy your next life; and the worse you do in this life, the lower grade incarnation you will receive in the next. This idea collapses on many levels. Those who hold to it fail to adequately explain *what* is reincarnated by *whom*, *how*, or *why*?

This is what the apostle John foresaw in his heavenly vision:

> Then I saw a great white throne and him who was seated on it. The earth and the heavens fled from his presence, and there was no place for them. And I saw the dead, great and small, standing before the throne, and books were opened. Another book was opened, which is the book of life. The dead were judged according to what they had done as recorded in the books. The sea gave up

the dead that were in it, and death and Hades gave up the dead that were in them, and each person was judged according to what they had done" (Rev. 20:11-13).

This is proof that the Day of Judgment is fixed in God's calendar and unavoidable for every man, woman, and child. The only defense anyone can make as to *why* God should let them into Heaven would be based exclusively upon what Christ Jesus has done on their behalf. Expressed along the lines of "I submit to and celebrate the Lordship of Jesus Christ Who saved me! I plead the blood of the Lamb of God!" (See John 1:7, 29).

Blood Atonement

Animals had been offered as blood sacrifices ever since Adam and Eve stepped out of Eden, clothed in the skin of an animal God had prepared for them (Gen. 3:21). That sacrifice was to remind them that they needed a Savior. Sacrifices continued to be offered by the faithful during the centuries leading up to the giving of the Law through Moses (approximately sixteen hundred years B.C). Then, in God's Law, many specifics were given concerning the sacrifices that needed to be offered—for example, where, by whom, how, and why (especially detailed in the book of Leviticus).

Then came Christ, God's Provision, the One Whom all sacrifices beforehand had prefigured and Who would now fulfill their significance, as written: "Those sacrifices [were] an annual reminder of sins. It is impossible for the blood of bulls and goats to take away sins . . . we have been made holy through the sacrifice of the body of Jesus Christ once for all" (Heb. 10:3-4, 10). Our sin has been *atoned* for. We are brought together in Christ (*at-one-ment*) and made acceptable to God. In fact, the whole letter to the Hebrews teaches this amazing truth.

But Why Does God Save Some and Not Others?

There are so many ways to distract yourself from contemplating your inevitable death—some legitimate, like work, family, home, sleep, sport, entertainment and some illegitimate, such as drugs, drunkenness, gambling, adultery, or even overindulgence in some off the legitimate list. But at the same time, for a number of people, life is just too hard and too unpleasant; and they fantasize about ending it all themselves. The toughest question some have to make in life is whether or not to end it. An honest atheist would do just that if they acted in conformity with their convictions—to escape a world of pointless pain and to silence their immaterial conscience lest it expose them. So, why don't they?

Ironically, they agree that the pursuit of pleasure has value and, therefore, prefer existence over non-existence, even though they fail to provide any rational reason to qualify their conclusions. In truth, they fear death—which is irrational according to their evolutionary worldview—because they fear being confronted by the God they deny, before Whom they know they cannot excuse themselves. But what of those who do take their own life? In their case, to be clear, it was taken from them. God hardened their hearts by giving them over to their own self-destructive passions (Rom. 1:18-32).

Yet there are those whom God has promised never to let go (Deut. 31:6; Matt. 28:20). Maybe you are one of them, one whom God is pursuing, one to whom He is revealing Himself. The same God Who commanded, "'Let light shine out of darkness,' made His light shine in our hearts to give us the light of the knowledge of God's glory displayed in the face of Christ" (2 Cor. 4:6). Some might ask, "Why does God save only some people and not everyone?" But a more profound question would be, "Why does God save anyone at all?"

The answer could be illustrated with a picture, called "God's Glory," viewed from two perspectives. One perspective is up close and personal, while the other is all-encompassing. Although the near-view is awe-inspiring, it appears to be, at times, incongruent and perplexing, at which point, some are in danger of misunderstanding the mind and will of God and of losing their footing. These are those who do not have a firm grip upon God's Word. It is easy for them to fall into the quicksand of error, even heresy (which is to deny a central Gospel truth). But if we persistently begin with God's Word and apply our God-given faith, then as we peer through the haze and scan the horizon, we can begin to make sense of the diversity and unity, pain and pleasure, depravity and beauty that we see in the cosmos. And we can begin to embrace and delight in the reason for everything: "God's glory."

The Apex and the Reason for Everything

The only true and invisible God has clothed Himself with creation that we may know Him and enjoy Him forever. Intrinsically, God is holy, other, eternal, and infinite and transcends all that He has made, sustaining everything by the power of His word, which resides in Him as we considered in chapter two. And when He puts Himself on display, that which is knowable and, at times tangible, is His glory!

This is why it is necessary for a holy God to judge a sin-cursed creation by fire and to plunge all who stand opposed to Him into eternal punishment in Hell (2 Peter 3). While at the same time, due to His own compassion and mercy and not someone's self-righteousness, merit, or intrinsic worth, God chooses to save a people "to the praise of his glorious grace" (Eph. 1:6). God has quite a lot to say about all this in His Word:

- "What then shall we say? Is God unjust? Not at all! For he says to Moses, 'I will have mercy on whom I have mercy, and I will have compassion on whom I have compassion.' It does not, therefore, depend on human desire or effort, but on God's mercy" (Rom. 9:14-16).
- "But who are you, a human being, to talk back to God?" (Rom. 9:20).
- "Oh, the depth of the riches of the wisdom and knowledge of God! How unsearchable his judgments, and his paths beyond tracing out! 'Who has known the mind of the Lord? Or who has been his counselor?' 'Who has ever given to God, that God should repay them?' For from him and through him and for him are all things. To him be the glory forever! Amen" (Rom. 11:33-36).
- "It is because of him that you are in Christ Jesus, who has become for us wisdom from God—that is, our righteousness, holiness and redemption. Therefore, as

it is written: 'Let the one who boasts boast in the Lord'" (1 Cor. 1:30-31).

Jesus is our Peace, our Hope, our Joy. Now, the way of salvation back to God is open. But from what are we saved? We are saved from God's holy wrath. He would otherwise justly condemn us, along with everyone else who is unholy and saturated with sin. Amazingly, we are saved from eternal punishment in Hell, where Christ, not Satan, reigns (Matt. 16:18, 28:18; Rev. 1:18, 20:10, 14).

We are also saved from our own deceiving and self-indulgent hearts, which formerly desired only to dethrone God and lay claim to His glory. We are now free from suffocating guilt, cancerous hate, and the hopeless dissatisfaction from pursuing transient and lustful pleasure. And as this salvation is through faith in Christ Jesus alone, it is absolute and fully dependable. It is according to His righteousness that we are accepted and privileged to be called children of God (1 John 3:1-5; Rom. 8:15-17). As those ransomed, healed, restored, and forgiven, we are eternally secure because of Jesus and His finished, crucial, cross-centered work: "Blessed is the one whose transgressions are forgiven, whose sins are covered. Blessed is the one whose sin the LORD does count against them and in whose spirit is no deceit" (Psalm 32:1-2).

So Why Was the Law of God Given to Moses and the People of Israel?

This is something that the vast majority of Jewish people have struggled to comprehend for centuries, along with all who fall prey to legalism (salvation by works). They fail to understand that the Law of Moses given thirty-five hundred years ago was designed to display God's standard of perfection, which He cannot compromise without denying His own justice. It was also given to highlight our failure to measure up to His perfection. And so, to point us to Christ, the One Who came in human flesh to fulfill every command of God on our behalf (Gal. 4:24).

Yes, the Jew was to obey and practice the Law to *prove* their love for God, and we are also called to adhere to those same timeless principles. But they were never to rely on *their* love for God to be saved, but in *His* love for them, for those whom Christ came to save. This is the main lesson to be learned when Jesus is confronted by the rich, young ruler in Mark 10:17-31.

Therefore, we conclude that the ceremonial laws were only ever meant to be temporary, until Christ fulfilled them (Gal. 3:23-25; Heb. 10). And why the civil laws were exclusively for the nation of Israel; every nation has variations. Whereas the moral laws—based upon the character of God, Whose principles are to be adhered to no matter which culture or age in which you are living—are for us also. This is why when Jesus taught and applied these laws, He internalized them, showing how they may very well have been broken at a heart level, although they may appear to have been kept outwardly (Matt. 5-7, 22:34-40).

In an earlier chapter, we have already considered the battle that Martin Luther, a medieval monk-turned-Christian reformer, waged to try to attain his own righteousness. The battle nearly killed him as he attempted to rigorously keep religious practices and holy observances that he thought might please God. He finally rested on the words, "For in the gospel a righteousness from God is revealed—a righteousness that is by faith from first to last, just as it is written, 'The righteous will live by faith'" (Rom. 1:17).

Nothing to Boast About

This demolishes pride! There is nothing in us of which to boast. There is nothing we can point to in us and say, "Look at me, God! Consider my good works! Consider my worthiness! I've earned Your love! I deserve it! Now accept me!"

I hope that will be nothing like your plea to God on the final day. Be warned: God has already told us how He will respond to such people. "'I never knew you. Away from me, you evildoers!'" (Matt. 7:23). "'There is no one who is righteous, not even one'" (Rom 3:10, cf. Psalm 14:1-3). "All of us have become like one who is unclean, and all our righteous acts are like filthy rags" (Isa. 64:6). (Although many translators opt for "filthy rags," the Hebrew is even more offensive and should be more accurately translated as "used menstrual cloth").

In the book of Galatians, the apostle Paul rebukes the church of Galatia in the strongest way that the Greek language could afford him (Gal. 1:8-9, 3:1, 5:12). After beginning with confidence in Christ to save, they had allowed themselves to be deceived into thinking that they could finish the work themselves!

Let me illustrate the terrible conflict that can emerge and threaten to overwhelm even those who are truly the Lord's as we can be tempted to listen to the accusations of the evil one, who seeks to rob us of our peace with God and the appreciation of our secure position in Christ.

A Terrible Conflict

The following citations are taken from John Bunyan's autobiographical book, Grace Abounding to the Chief of Sinners,[95] written in 1666, which, in many ways, lay the ground for The Pilgrim's Progress written twelve years later.

This is the struggle that John Bunyan, the Puritan preacher who wrote "The Pilgrim's Progress" in 1678, had for a number of years *after* he was saved; although his troubled conscience began to plague him even *before* his conversion. While still utterly lost in the world, "taking much delight in all manner of vice," he recalls, "a voice did suddenly dart from heaven into my soul, which said, 'Wilt thou leave thy sins and go to heaven, or have thy sins and go to hell?'" He was quick to conclude, "I had been a great and grievous sinner, and that it was now too late for me to look after heaven; for Christ would not forgive me, nor pardon my transgression . . . I felt my heart sink into despair."

Then foolishly, Bunyan decided, "I can but be damned, and if I must be so, I had as good be damned for many sins, as to be damned for few." And this became his code of conduct:

> I went on in sin with greediness of mind, still clutching that I could not be so satisfied with it as I would. This did continue with me about a month, or more; but one day, as I was standing at a neighbors[sic] shop window, and there cursing and swearing, and playing the madman, after my wonted manner, there sat within

---

[95] John Bunyan, *Grace Abounding to the Chief of Sinners* (London: George Larkin, 1666).

the woman of the house, and heard me, who, though she was a very loose and ungodly wretch, yet protested that I swore and cursed at that most fearful rate, that she was made to tremble to hear me; and told me further, that I was the ungodliest fellow for swearing that ever she heard in all her life; and that I, by this doing, was able to spoil all the youth in a whole town, if they came but in my company.

Later on, he did try, oh so hard, to shake off his wicked nature and silence his forked tongue, but his efforts always seemed to fall short and give him no solace. "Poor wretch as I was, I was all this while ignorant of Jesus Christ, and going about to establish my own righteousness; and had perished therein, had not God, in mercy, showed me more of my state of nature."

What helped enormously was a conversation he overheard. "Four poor women sitting at a door in the sun, and talking about the things of God." He tells us what happened:

> I drew near to hear what they said . . . Their talk was about a new birth, the work of God on their hearts, also how they were convinced of their miserable state by nature, they talked how God had visited their souls with His love in the Lord Jesus, and with what words and promises they have been refreshed, comforted, and supported against the temptations of the devil . . . and how they were borne up under His assaults. They also discoursed of their own wretchedness of heart, of their unbelief; and did condemn, slight, and abhor

their own righteousness, as filthy and insufficient to do them any good.

The majority of Bunyan's autobiographical book is about how he fought continuously with his conscience and the devil. He wrestled with condemning passages in the Bible about those who may have once showed signs of salvation but were ultimately lost and stories of those who were beyond salvation completely, no matter how much they appeared to pursue it. He felt this was most clearly and hauntingly illustrated by the life of Esau, who, after selling his rights as the firstborn for a stew, was tricked out of his father's blessing years later and was unable to retrieve it even with many tears (Gen. 25:29-34, 27:1-46; Heb. 12:16-17).

Nervous Breakdown

Bunyan believed that the despised firstborn rights represented salvation, and the latter blessing represented peace with God. Bunyan almost suffered a nervous breakdown as he agonized in his spirit that, surely, he, like Esau, would lose his salvation and be ultimately rejected by God. Bunyan even convinced himself for a long, painful season that he had committed the unforgivable sin (Mark 3:20-35; Matt. 12; Luke 12:1-12), and that after much resistance, he had finally succumbed to the devil's temptation to deny Christ. And therefore, there was no way back. He confessed:

> All my comfort was taken from me, then darkness seized upon me, after which whole floods of blasphemies, both

against God, Christ, and the Scriptures, were poured upon my spirit, to my great confusion and astonishment. These blasphemous thoughts were such as so stirred up questions in me, against the very being of God, and of His only beloved Son; as whether there were in truth, a God, or Christ, or no? And whether the holy Scriptures were not rather a fable, and cunning story, then a holy and pure Word of God?

[The temptation was to] sell Christ for this, or sell Christ for that; sell Him, sell Him . . . The temptation lay upon me for a space of a year, and did follow me so continually that I was not rid of it one day in a month, no, not sometimes one hour in many days together, unless when I was asleep . . .

[Then, finally, one terrible day], I felt this thought pass through my heart, "Let Him go, if He will!" and I thought also, that I felt my heart freely consent thereto. Oh, the diligence of Satan! Oh, the desperateness of man's heart! Now was the battle won, and down I fell as a bird that is shot from the top of a tree, into great guilt, and fearful despair . . . I was like a man bereft of life, and as now past all recovery, and bound over to eternal punishment.

Guilt and What to Do About It

Oh, poor Bunyan! This was his problem—his sense of guilt and what to do with it. He had tried so hard to know God, to serve Him faithfully, to live according to that which pleased Him; but he knew that he had failed. He had let his Lord down. Now, he was plagued and harassed by his sense of guilt, which drew him further from the Lord and into a downward spiral of depression.

At this time, I must ask you also: What do you do with your guilt? Not just your guilty feelings, but also the reality of your conscious awareness of your guilt before a holy God, against Whom you have sinned? What Bunyan needed to better understand at that time was what we considered earlier—that the redemptive soul-saving work of Jesus is a *finished* and altogether *sufficient* work, able to save and to *keep* saved all who look to Jesus as their Savior. Some of the last words that Jesus uttered as He died on the cross were, "'It is finished!'" (John 19:30).

Every religion in the world and every sect who call themselves Christian but deny some of the essential doctrines that must be believed to be saved try to mix what we ought to do with what some Divine personages do to secure our salvation, whereas, true biblical Christianity affirms that Jesus has done it all and left us nothing to do but believe. "If you declare with your mouth, 'Jesus is Lord,' and believe in your heart that God raised Him from the dead, you will be saved" (Rom. 10:9).

Referring to Jesus' saving work on earth and continuing preserving prayers in Heaven, the writer to the Hebrews affirms, "He is able to save completely those who come to God through him, because he always lives to intercede for them" (Heb. 7:25). While still on earth, Jesus said, "'I shall lose none of all those [the Father] has given me, but raise them up at the last day. For my Father's will is that everyone who looks to the Son and believes in him shall have eternal life, and I will raise them up at the last day'" (John 6:39-40).

Our Assurance Guaranteed

Please, dear reader, take time to savor the awesome truth that *nothing* in all creation—past, present, or future—can "separate us from the love of God that is in Christ Jesus our Lord" (Rom. 8:39). Eternal life is granted to all the followers of Jesus—not *temporary* life, not the *possibility* of eternal life, but the *certainty* of it. This is why the apostle John wrote his letter, 1 John. "I write these things to you who believe in the name of the Son of God so that you may *know* that you *have* eternal life" (1 John 5:13, italics mine).

Bunyan must have known the above verses, but he didn't apply them to his own desperate situation for many months and so was heavy-laden with his guilt and full of sorrow. Until, he records, "Suddenly this sentence bolted in upon me, 'The blood of Christ remits all guilt.' At this I made a stand in my spirit; with that, this word took hold upon me, 'the blood of Jesus, [God's] Son, purifies us from all sin.' Now I began to conceive peace in my soul, and methought I saw as if the tempter did leer and steal away from me."

Feelings and Emotions Can Deceive

He would still have moments of doubt and spiritual depression but only when he forgot these truths, took his eyes off the Savior, turned to his own wayward and self-deceiving heart. As the prophet Jeremiah warned, "The heart is deceitful above all things and beyond cure. Who can understand it?" (Jer. 17:9).

That is why our heart, our feelings and emotions, our experiences, and even our ability to rationalize is not the standard and authority by which we measure truth. We must submit not only to a higher authority but to *the* highest authority: God and His inspired Word, which was written down by the prophets and apostles and preserved down through the centuries by the Spirit of God (2 Tim. 3:16).

I wish I could have met John Bunyan when he was going through one of those terrible guilt-ridden ordeals and to have pointed him to these two verses: "This is how we know that we belong to the truth and how we set our hearts at rest in His presence: If our hearts condemn us, we know that God is greater than our hearts, and he knows everything" (1 John. 3:19-20). I hope you find consolation in those words, too.

God's Glory Guaranteed

As we come to the end of this chapter, meditate on this: your salvation and assurance is not about you! It's not about your comfort, your peace, your sense of fulfillment, your rescue—not primarily. That might be a shock to some. It is about God's glory, revealed through the life, death, and resurrection of Christ Jesus! He is central in God's plan and purpose. It is about God revealing Himself in space and time—and yes, also through your life and experience—that you might join in the angelic chorus and sing, "'Worthy is the Lamb, who was slain, to receive power and wealth and wisdom and strength and honor and glory and praise!' . . . every creature in heaven and on earth and under the earth and on the sea, and all that is in them [saying]: 'To Him who sits on the throne and to the Lamb be praise and honor and glory and power, for ever and ever!'" (Rev. 5:12-13).

We should not primarily be pursuing emotional rest, a transcendental experience, intellectual satisfaction, nor even spiritual pleasure but to appropriately worship God the Father, through God the Son, by God the Spirit, as the Triune God Who has chosen to reveal Himself generally in creation and specifically in the Bible. We must raise our gaze from our navels and our wallowing to the majestic King of kings, the triumphant Lord of lords, the God of glory!

Rest Assured

The reason for everything is that God is revealing Himself to be altogether glorious that we may "worship [Him] in the Spirit and in truth" (John 4:24). Only then can we fulfill the purpose for our existence as true worshippers (John 4:24). Only then can we enjoy the assured rest for our souls, knowing that we have been saved *by* the Almighty and *for* the Almighty. "For from him and through him and to him are all things. To him be the glory forever! Amen" (Rom. 11:36).

CHAPTER 9
The God Who Gives Hope

The excerpts in this chapter are taken from Joni Eareckson Tada's testimony, "A Deeper Healing."[96]

What follows is a window into the transformed life of one of the greatest living heroes of the faith—a story of one who has suffered more than most. Yet due to God's grace in her life, she has a hope which shines more brightly than most, even as she reflects God's glory which radiates through her broken clay vessel (2 Cor. 4:6-7).

Life or Death?

Joni Eareckson Tada is the author of around fifty books, she has produced fifteen albums of music, painted hundreds of paintings, been involved in countless radio broadcasts and TV programs, been featured in seven films, spoken at conferences all over the world, and runs a company which employs 150 employees and recruits over five thousand volunteers annually. Oh, and she has also been a quadriplegic for over fifty years!

---

96 Times Square Church, "|Guest| Joni Eareckson Tada | A Deeper Healing," September 24, 2017, YouTube video, 40:44, https://youtu.be/1AP2jeUVt6Y.

It was 1967 when her life changed forever. This is her story: "I took a dive into shallow waters . . . I broke my neck, and they told me that I would never walk again, never use my hands." She was seventeen years old and admits, "I plummeted into depression."

When her teenage friends would visit her, some would offer to read the Bible, while others would offer her alcohol to get drunk together. She tried to convince them to end her life, but all refused. She tried careening her motorized wheelchair into walls in the hope that she might break her neck completely, sever her airway, and suffocate. She remembers:

> I think back on those dark days and the hospital when I wanted so badly to cry . . . I would imagine myself lying on a mat next to an invalid who had been paralyzed for thirty-eight years that Jesus healed, hoping that Jesus would touch me, heal me, rescue me. Jesus . . . I don't want to spend the rest of my life without my hands or my legs . . . Please, Jesus . . . But as often as I prayed, I never got out of that wheelchair.

Joni went to a so-called "healing meeting," where hundreds of people gathered around a famous healer. But after an hour or so of music and testimonies, when some people were supposedly healed, she was still left in her wheelchair.

> But the spotlight never came to the wheelchair section, where the really hard cases were. Then we were ushered out early, so as not to cause a traffic jam at the elevator. I

was sitting there, number fifteen in a long line of thirty-five disabled people with crutches or wheelchairs, with white canes... and I'm thinking to myself... what kind of Savior—what kind of Deliverer—would refuse the prayers of people with disabilities, people like me? Ok, I thought resolutely, if God's not going to heal me, then I'm not going to do this. I'm not going to live this way. Soon a bitter root—a real spirit of complaining—began to grip hold of my heart.

She returned to her sister's house, where she refused visitors and where she lay for two weeks in darkness, waiting to die. "Then an old hymn came up from my background. 'Abide with me: fast falls the eventide; the darkness deepens; Lord, with me abide. When other helpers fail, and comforts flee, Help of the helpless, O abide with me.' And finally, I cried out: 'God, if I can't die—and I want so badly to die—but if I can't, then, You are gonna have to be the One to show me how to live.'"

A little later, when flipping franticly through the Scriptures for answers using a stick placed in her mouth to turn the pages, she settled in Mark chapter one. There, large crowds gathered where Jesus was staying, but no one could find Him as He had woken early and gone to a solitary place to pray. When He returned, His disciples tried to rebuke Him, implying that He didn't care. He responded, "'Let's go somewhere else—to the nearby villages—so I can preach there also. That is why I have come'" (Mark 1:38). This was an inspiring moment for Joni:

> And that's when it hit me. It wasn't that Jesus did not care about all those disabled and diseased people. No, it's

just that their physical problems weren't His *main* focus. The Gospel was His focus. The Gospel says that sin kills; Hell is real, but God is merciful. His kingdom can change you, and Jesus is your Passport. And whenever people miss this, whenever people only came to Jesus just to get their physical problems fixed, that's when the Savior would back away . . . And that's when I started searching the Scriptures for a different kind of healing, a deeper kind of healing . . . For the last fifty years in this wheelchair, that's been my prayer.

A Deeper Kind of Healing

The *deeper healing* she speaks about is one of true sanctification, when the Spirit of God so works in a person as to drive out the desire for sin and selfishness and implants a desire for holiness and to serve Christ with whatever ability and opportunity that a person has. Yes, Joni still prayed for healing, for a miracle to get up and walk and return to having a *normal* life. But gradually, she was coming to realize that though God could heal her, He had chosen otherwise. He had something better in store for her. And *she* wasn't the focus of God's plan and purpose—*He* was. God would be increasingly glorified through her, in spite of more than fifty years as a quadriplegic.

From conception to natural death, regardless of disability in mind or body, every human being has equal dignity. God made plant life, the animal kingdom, the angelic host, and the human race. The world is our home, with plants and animals designed to help us enjoy it; and angels are sent to administer to the Christian's daily needs (Heb. 3:14). We, however, are neither animals nor angels but have the highest privilege—to be creatures made in God's image (Gen. 1:27).

Unlike animals, we were designed to be self-aware and, therefore, not only able to make rational and moral decisions but also to be responsible for them. We have been endowed by God to be creative and commanded to be fruitful, as we fulfill our duty by having dominion over the earth (Gen. 1:28).

From the beginning, God purposed that we share His likeness. That is, we are able to act with selfless love and to experience true joy, which is different to happiness, as that is circumstantial. We are able to be peacemakers—displaying patience, kindness, and goodness—in the face of hostility. We can discern God's will and act faithfully in obedience to His commands. We can even be meek, which is not a sign of weakness as some might propose but takes enormous strength of character. All of these characteristics are aspects of self-control (see Gal. 5:22-23).

While animals act instinctively, responding to the external forces imposed upon them, the Christian's self-control arises from the inner working of the Spirit of God. Tragically, this image of God in us is marred by our sinful, fallen nature (Gal. 5:19-21). That's why we must be born again by the Spirit of God (John 3). Then we may put our trust in Jesus as Savior and submit to His Lordship, and steadily, under the abiding influence of the Spirit, be transformed as He renews our minds and conforms us into the perfect image of Christ (Rom. 8).

God's Eternal Decree

> [Jesus Christ], being in very nature God, did not consider equality with God something to be used to his own advantage; rather, he made himself nothing by taking the very nature of a servant, being made in human likeness. And being found in appearance as a man, he humbled himself by becoming obedient to death—even death on a cross! Therefore God exalted him to the highest place and gave him the name that is above every name, that at the name of Jesus every knee should bow, in heaven and on earth and under the earth, and every tongue acknowledge that Jesus Christ is Lord, to the glory of God the Father (Phil. 2:6-11).

We need to accept our limitations and trials and learn to rejoice in our weaknesses and struggles (2 Cor. 12:9-10 and 1:9-11). We should recognize them as divinely sent prompts, as God teaches us to depend upon Him, here and now, while at the same time preparing us for future glory. Joni applies this line of reasoning to herself:

> God is always searching, always testing, and my weakness—my physical weakness, my physical problems—are the very thing that He uses to expose what needs to be changed in my life. When we are weak, our defenses are down. The cracks in our character show ... the not-so-pretty stuff of which I am made. Suffering is the textbook that will teach you to know who you really are ... We try to ignore weaknesses ... We're embarrassed by them ... We don't want to talk about them. We try to hide them. We don't like suffering. We

try to drug it, medicate it, surgically exorcise it, divorce it, institutionalize it, do anything but live with it."

Quoting Andrew Murray,[97] Joni recites the following:

> "God wants us to rest and even rejoice in weakness... It is the secret of strength and success. It is our weakness heartily accepted and continually realized that gives us our access to the strength of Him who said, '*My grace is sufficient for you, for my power is made perfect in weakness.*'" The weaker I was, the more I learned to lean on Jesus; and the more I leaned on Jesus, the stronger I discovered Him to be.

A "Splash-Over of Hell"

Then in 2010, Joni was diagnosed with Stage Three breast cancer, as well as beginning to suffer from chronic pain. She remembers a conversation returning from a chemotherapy session. While her husband drove with her strapped down in the back of the car, she said to him:

> Suffering—it's like little splash-overs of Hell, waking you up out of your spiritual slumber and getting you to seriously appreciate the actual Hell from which Christ has rescued the Christian... Then we started wondering, "What are splash-overs of Heaven? Are they when all the

---

[97] Andrew Murray was a nineteenth century African writer, teacher, and preacher.

bills are paid, and there are no aches and pains, and the sun is bright on the horizon, and everyone is happy and smiling? No, no, I don't think so. I think a splash-over of Heaven is finding Jesus in your splash-over of Hell. Jesus, Jesus is your Ecstasy beyond compare. And when you're suffering, there's no one better to go to, then One Who was hung like meat on a hook. He knows suffering. He wrote the book on suffering. And when you draw near to Him . . . oh, the sweetness, oh the ecstasy, oh the joy, the tenderness, the loveliness, the beauty of the Lord Jesus Christ . . . and it is worth anything, anything, to be His friend.

From Glory to Glory

With her face radiant with a Gospel glow, Joni said:

I am so looking forward to Heaven. There will be praise songs for all of eternity . . . "by His grace, I shall look on His face; that shall be glory, glory for me . . . " I want to step into that design that God created me to be long before eternity . . . because Heaven is coming, and I will have a new heart, not just a new body. Don't be thinking that the body is the main focus. Like I said, I'm into the *deeper healing*; I'm looking for the new heart—a glorified heart that no longer twists the truth . . . a heart that no longer resists God and looks for an escape or gets defeated easily by doubt, or worry, or anxiety. A heart that doesn't try to justify itself by feeling sorry for itself. That will be Heaven for me. On that day, God is going to close the curtain on sin and suffering and Satan . . . and the appearance of the Lord Jesus is gonna be so amazing that it will suffice for all your hurts and mine, and it will atone for every single one of your tears. Then God is gonna lift the veil, the curtain on our five senses, and we will see the whole universe in plain sight. And I can't wait for that day when I can hopefully, hopefully, I don't know, take this wheelchair to Heaven, and I'll put it right over there. Then, with my brand-new glorified body and heart, I'm going to stand next to Jesus. And I will take His hand in mine—I can't feel my hand; I haven't felt anyone touch it for fifty years—but then I will feel His hand in mine. I will feel His nail scars where He bled for me. And I will say, "Jesus, You were right when You said in this life we will have trouble. Because in this life [pointing at the wheelchair], that thing was a lot of trouble. The weaker I was in that thing, the harder I leaned upon you. And the harder I leaned upon you, the stronger I discovered you to be. Jesus, thank you."

So, now we live in the last of the last days, awaiting Christ's glorious return (Acts 1:11; Jude 14-15), when He will raise all the dead, some unto everlasting judgment, others with saving faith in Him to everlasting glory. And He will reward us according to what we have done (Rev. 22:12). This is a good cue to think about what you are doing for Him—not *have done* or *plan to do* but *are doing*. Would you have any regrets if you died today? Would you ask for more time, to go back to get busy with His business? Well, here you are. What are you going to do *now* while you still have time?

Christ has promised to return! When He does, He will gather up His people; restore all things to an even more glorious state than before the Fall, and abide with the saints forever (John 14:1-4; Rev. 21; Isa. 65:17; Eph. 1:9-10). God even affirms this from His very throne in the apostle John's vision. "'Look! God's dwelling place is now among the people, and he will dwell with them. They will be his people, and God himself will be with them and be their God. *He will wipe every tear from their eyes. There will be no more death*, or mourning or crying or pain, for the old order of things has passed away'" (Rev. 21:3-4).

Are you ready to meet with your Creator? Are you trusting in Christ's perfect righteousness, in nothing more or less than Jesus' shed blood on the cross in payment for your sin that you might be eternally united with Him? "Since, then, you have been raised with Christ, set your hearts on things above, where Christ is, seated at the right hand of God. Set your minds on things above, not on earthly things. For you died, and your life is now hidden with Christ in God. When Christ, who is your life, appears, then you also will appear with him in glory" (Col. 3:1-4). Along with Joni, and all the saints that are featured in this book: I can't wait. Are you ready?

APPENDIX A
The Origin of Evil Explored

There are people who claim that God must be a myth because of the reality of evil. But this is a nonsensical statement because if there were no God, there would be no ultimate standard by which to measure and to conclude that anything is either good or evil. Even so, let's consider that objection. If God exists, why do bad things happen to good people? Of course, this question could be turned around. If God doesn't exist, why do good things happen to bad people?

Intrinsically, there are no good people. "'There is no one righteous, not even one . . . there is no one who does good, not even one'" (Rom. 3:10-12, cf. Psalm 14). Jesus affirms, "'No one is good—except God alone'" (Mark 10:18). Goodness is an attribute of God which is communicated to His children once adopted through faith in Jesus (Rom. 3:22). Until we recognize our need for Jesus and trust in His sufficiency to save us, we are all considered as lost sinners who have fallen short of God›s holy standard, and as such, no one can be considered good. We are all, essentially, bad people. Yet there is a legitimate heart to the objectors' question, which could be framed this way: if God is altogether good and created everything good, then how could anything become bad? What is the origin of evil?

Man's "Fall"

God tells us Himself that He created everything and stated that it was good (Gen. 1). However, soon afterwards, man, once considered by God to be "very good," developed evil desires which led to evil thoughts, followed by evil actions. When did this happen? No one knows for sure. But it was likely to have been shortly after the creation week and before the conception of Cain and Abel, their first children.

Adam and Eve disobeyed God. "The LORD God commanded the man, 'You are free to eat from any tree in the garden; but you must not eat from the tree of the knowledge of good and evil, for when you eat from it you will certainly die'" (Gen. 2:16-17). Tragically, our first parents ignored God's warning and broke His law. Adam and Eve's spiritual death was immediate, demonstrated by awareness of their nakedness and confirmed by their separation from God's gracious communion as they were expelled from Eden. Then, a few centuries later, they also suffered physical death (Gen. 5:5).

Satan's "Fall"

Interestingly, man's fall on earth followed the pattern that Satan had already carved out in Heaven, once "blameless in [his] ways . . . till wickedness was found in [him]" (Ezek. 28:15). Although Ezekiel 28 is first and foremost an indictment against the king of Tyre, it uses Satan's proud fall as a type of parable to emphasize the king's imminent fall, also due to pride. It is obvious that Satan's experience is being referenced as a warning as he was "in Eden, the garden of God" (Ezek. 28:13). Then, we have this fascinating verse: "You were blameless in your ways from the day you were created till wickedness was found in you... and you sinned. So I drove you in disgrace from the mount of God, and I expelled you, guardian cherub... Your heart became proud on account of your beauty, and you corrupted your wisdom because of your splendor. So I threw you to the earth" (Ezek. 28:15-17).

In Isaiah 14:4-23, judgment is being voiced primarily against another king, Nebuchadnezzar of Babylon, whose wicked thoughts are likened to that of Satan. "How you have fallen from heaven, morning star, son of the dawn! You have been cast down to the earth ... You said in your heart, 'I will ascend to the heavens; I will raise my throne above the stars of God . . . I will make myself like the Most High.' But you are brought down to the realm of the dead, to the depths of the pit" (Isa. 14:12-15).

In Luke 10:18, Jesus says to His disciples, "'I saw Satan fall like lightning from heaven.'" In Revelation 12, we have a review of Satan's fall, his attack upon the Lord Jesus, then of the war he wages against all Christians. Remember that this is told using figurative and highly symbolic language. When did Satan rebel and get cast out of Heaven? No one can say for sure but sometime after the Creation week and before Adam and Eve sinned.

Now let us take the origin of evil question one layer deeper. From where and how did the *desire* for evil originate? Wasn't Satan formerly an angel of light who would have enjoyed God's glorious presence in Heaven? Didn't Adam and Eve walk with God in the garden of paradise on earth? How could their hearts have become corrupted and evil thoughts overwhelm them?

We must always tread carefully where God has not specifically shed His revelatory light upon an answer to our questions. We would be wise not to be too dogmatic with our conclusions and to be aware of the constant danger of manipulating or undermining what God has clearly revealed elsewhere in Scripture simply to fit our thesis.

While conscious of the above, God has given us inquiring minds, which may profit from asking such profound questions if we attempt to investigate possible answers by drawing upon what we *do* know of God's character and will, with the desire that God be glorified in all things. Though both the angelic host and the human race were created and considered by God to be "good," it seems reasonable to conclude that they also had the ability to sin. Even so, they always obeyed as the outworking of their good desire to do so, under the good influence and wise direction of God.

Meanwhile, along with the great authority that God had assigned to Lucifer, He had also attributed him with beauty, which was to be enjoyed by all the angels, as well as by God. Until, to fulfill God's Sovereign purposes, He withdrew His good influence and wise direction from Lucifer. Now contrary, evil thoughts began to overwhelm him, as his formerly good desire to worship God became corrupt. Without any external restraining factor, the good void was inevitably filled with sinful pride. Now a new desire for self-adoration became insatiable; for pride leads only to dissatisfaction and resentment, which in turn spawns envy. God had what Lucifer now desired for himself—worship. Lucifer would have known then—as it has also been made explicit in the Scriptures since—that no one—neither man, nor angel, nor anything in all creation—is to be worshipped but God alone (Acts 12:21-23, 14:8-18; Rev. 19:10, 22:8-9; Rom. 1:21-25).

Have you ever heard the saying, "Nature abhors a vacuum"? This is true and can also be applied to spiritual realities.[98] Without light, there

---

98 Matthew 12:22-28, 30, 43-45

can only be darkness; without sound, only silence; without motion, stillness. Similarly, where goodness is withheld, evil fills the void.

Evil Is Uncreated

But let it be understood clearly that God did not create evil. Evil is not a created thing; it is immaterial, without substance or being. It is a way of describing behavior, a response, which does not align with God's goodness and prescribed will. Although it is true that God ordained what was necessary for it to occur, God did this without violating Lucifer's will, which means that Lucifer is responsible for his own desires and actions. He has always been free to act according to his strongest desire, as is the case with every creature. Before "wickedness was found in [Lucifer]" (Ezek. 28:15), he desired to worship God. But when God withheld His good influence from him, evil became the most attractive choice; and without God's holy restraint, Lucifer chose to oppose God, even to be worshipped as God.

So, God cannot be accused of being the Author of evil or be blamed for it. He hates it! Evil is everything that is antithetical to God. And yet, evil is only possible when God willingly withholds or retracts His good influence and wise direction from those who perform it. But even this, God does in a measured way and for a *good* purpose, which we will come to in a moment.

Once cast to earth, although he knew he could not overpower God, Satan was determined to rob God of His enjoyment of man by undermining man's worship, especially as he coveted it for himself. Up until then, Adam and Eve had rightly desired to, literally, image

God as they enjoyed fellowship with Him. Satan now set out to corrupt their good desire by breeding dissatisfaction in them by encouraging them to doubt God's goodness and love, suggesting that He had withheld some good thing from them (Gen. 3:5).

This doubt chiseled away at their confidence in God and distorted their relationship with Him, even before they inevitably acted upon it. The good desire to want to be more *like* God, to become wiser, morphed into an evil desire to be *as* God. Now, they desired unauthorized wisdom, which they were forbidden to possess; pursuing this was to transgress, to step over the threshold into disobedience (Gen. 2:6). They broke the one law that God had clearly given to Adam (Gen. 2:17), and so together, they became lawbreakers—sinners.

Why Did God Permit Evil?

Why did God not intervene before this happened—not just before the first temptation on earth but even before the rebellion in Heaven? Why does God permit (even ordain) evil? (Eph. 1:3-14; Rom. 8:28-29; Lam. 3:37-39; Prov. 16:4; Isa. 46:10).

Amazingly, God utilizes the existence of evil to display the surpassing excellence and perfection of His holy being, which involved the humiliation and exaltation of His beloved Son, Jesus, Who ultimately conquered our sin, the spawn of evil, as the Last Adam, through perfect obedience as he "humbled Himself and became obedient to death—even death on a cross! Therefore, God exalted him to the highest place and gave him the name that is above every name, that at the name of Jesus every knee should bow, in heaven and on earth and under the earth, and every tongue acknowledge that Jesus Christ is Lord, to the glory of God the Father" (Phil. 2:8-11).[99]

In Eden, Adam and Eve could not fully appreciate God's love and goodness; they could not begin to understand His patience, faithfulness, mercy, justice, or grace—not until after their fall from grace and later restoration.

So, Who Is Responsible for Evil?

There is one final objection some might still put forth after all that has been presented and considered so far: If it was God's will to withdraw His *good* influence from Lucifer, Adam, and Eve, leaving them unable to do anything *good,* only to sin, why are they still held responsible? Or as others have similarly argued, "'Then why does God still blame us? For who is able to resist his will?'" (Rom. 9:19). God answers, through the apostle Paul:

> But who are you, a human being, to talk back to God? "Shall what is formed say to the one who formed it, 'Why did you make me like this?' Does not the potter have the right to make out of the same lump of clay some pottery for special purposes and some for common use? What if God, although choosing to show his wrath and make his power known, bore with great patience the objects of His wrath—prepared for destruction? What if he did this to make the riches of his glory known to the objects of his mercy, whom he prepared in advance for glory— (Rom. 9:20-23).

---

99   Philippians 2:5-11; Romans 5:20-21; 1 Corinthians 16:55-57

God does exactly as He pleases (Isa. 46:10b), "work[ing] out everything in conformity with the purpose of his will...for the praise of his glory" (Eph. 1:11-12). And He does not owe us an explanation; there are secret things known only to Himself (Deut. 29:29). Yes, there remains an element of mystery around this subject. But as far as He allows us to understand, it should instill in us a healthy fear of God, especially in light of what God has told us clearly: "'I will have mercy on whom I have mercy, and I will have compassion on whom I have compassion' (Rom. 9:15, cf. Exod. 33:19).

If you are a recipient of His mercy and compassion and, as a result, have been granted salvation through faith in Jesus Christ, may your sense of awe and reverence toward God grow and be expressed in worship that is pleasing to Him—"'in the Spirit and in truth'" (John 4:24).

APPENDIX B
What Is Eternity?

Most think about eternity as an unimaginable amount of time. But time and eternity are quite different. Time, as we have come to understand it, is finite, with a beginning and an end (Isa. 46:10), whereas eternity is a state of perpetual being. Time is also a means by which we observe change, even as we measure our own journey through life—which for most has a bumpy start and a lumpy finish. Also, time and eternity *largely* operate in two different dimensions, with eternity encapsulating time. I said *largely* as there is an overlap by degrees. To help illustrate both the magnitude and relationship between time and eternity, think of a microscopic particle enveloped by outer space.

There could very well be a sense in which time operates in eternity upon creatures for thoughts and motion to occur. And God has made us in such a way so as to have "set eternity in the human heart" (Eccl. 3:11), meaning that as rational beings we *all* know God exists and that there is more to life than the empirical here and now. Jesus affirms in His prayer to the Father, referring to the Christian believer, "Now this is eternal life: that they know you, the only true God, and Jesus Christ, whom you have sent" (John 17:3). He is not primarily referring to a quantity but a quality of life, enriched by fellowship with God Himself that can be enjoyed *now*, and that will never end.

Consider carefully what Jesus then goes on to say: "I have brought you glory on earth by finishing the work you gave me to do. And now, Father, glorify me in your presence with the glory I had with you before the world began" (John 17:4-5). Thirty-three years earlier, Jesus had passed from eternity into time; and He was about to return—but not before accomplishing everything necessary that those He came to save could follow after Him one day. Ultimately, everyone will enter into eternity, but not everyone will spend it enjoying God's glory forever. Only those who submit to Jesus' leading on earth will follow Him into Heaven.

Additional Resources

Answers in Genesis: answersingenesis.org.

Blanchard, John. *Does God Believe in Atheists?* Welwyn Garden City: EP Books, 2011.

Blanchard, John. *Whatever Happened to Hell?* Wheaton: Crossway Books, 1995.

Burgess, Stuart. *Hallmarks of Design: Evidence of Design in the Natural World.* Leominster: Day One Publications, 2005.

Chan, Francis. "Letters to the Church." Colorado Springs: David C. Cook, 2018.

Donnelly, Edward. *Heaven and Hell.* Edinburgh: Banner of Truth, 2001.

Godfrey, W. Robert. *Reformation Sketches.* Phillipsburg: P & R Publishing Company, 2012.

Heck, Charles. "Martin Luther: His Trip to Rome (1510)." WorldySaints blog. January 6, 2017. https://worldlysaints.wordpress.com/2017/01/06/martin-luther-his-trip-to-rome-1510.

Lightfoot, Neil R. *How We Got the Bible.* Grand Rapids: Baker Books, 2003.

McGrath, Alister. *The Dawkins Delusion: Atheist Fundamentalism and the Denial of the Divine*. Lisle: InterVarsity Press, 2010.

Mohler, Albert. "The Briefing." The Southern Baptist Theological Seminary. https://albertmohler.com/the-briefing.

Olyott, Stuart. "The Noncomformist Minister." In Robert Strivens, ed. *Which Church? How to Identify a Biblical Church*. Darlington: Evangelical Press, 2007.

Owen, John. *The Death of Death in the Death of Christ*. Edinburgh: Banner of Truth Trust, 1959.

Packer, J. I. *Knowing God*. Lisle: InterVarsity Press, 1993.

Pink, A. W. *The Sovereignty of God*. Woodstock: Watchmaker Publishing.

Ryle, J. C. *Holiness*. CreateSpace Independent Publishing, 2013.

Sproul, R. C. *The Holiness of God*. Sanford: Ligonier Ministries, 1986.

Tozer, A. W. *The Attributes of God*. Camp Hills: Wingspread Publishers, 2007.

Watson, Thomas. *A Body of Divinity*. Edinburgh: Banner of Truth Publishing, 1984.

Bibliography

Adelfred. "Little Richard—Little Richard's Testimony." YouTube. 2011. RadioBroadcast. 5:31. https://www.youtube.com/watch?v=l3jktkVg3lU.

Amsterdam, Peter. "More Like Jesus: Reflections on Faithfulness and Holiness." *Directors' Corner.* The Family International. June 16, 2020. https://directors.tfionline.com/post/more-jesus-reflections-faithfulness-and-holiness.

Anselm, St., Archbishop of Canterbury. Chapter II. *Prosologion.* Accessed November 7, 2024.

"Augustine of Hippo." *Christianity Today* online. August 8, 2008. https://www.christianitytoday.com/2008/08/augustine-of-hippo.

Augustine of Hippo. "Oh, God, to know you is life. To serve You . . . " Theysaidso.com. Accessed June 7, 2024. https://theysaidso.com/quote/augustine-of-hippo-oh-god-to-know-you-is-life-to-serve-you-is-freedom-to-praise.

Augustine. "Sermon 73A." *Sermons.* Vol. III. Brooklyn: New City Press, 1991.

Augustine. "The Brambles of Lust." *Lapham's Quarterly.* Accessed November 10, 2024. https://www.laphamsquarterly.org/eros/brambles-lust.

Augustine. Chapter 12. *Confessions of Saint Augustine*. Vol. 9. London: Penguin Books, 1961.

Augustine. *Confessions*. Trans. Rex Warner. New York: Mentor, 1963.

Augustine. *Confessions*. Trans. F.J. Sheed. London: Penguin Classics, 2008.

Brecht, Martin and James Schaaf. *Martin Luther: His Road to Reformation 1483-1521*. Vol. 1. Minneapolis: Fortress Press, 1981.

Bunyan, John. *Grace Abounding to the Chief of Sinners*. London: George Larkin, 1666.

Elder, Fr. Joseph Mary. "Stigmata of St. Francis: 3 Ways for Holiness." Capuchins. September 13, 2017. https://www.capuchins.org/posts/stigmata-of-st-francis-3-ways-for-holiness.

Harris, Antipas L. *Holy Living: Toward A Practical Theology*. Eugene: Wipf and Stock, 2013.

"Incredible: Christian vs. Atheist Debate (White & Durbin vs Clark & Ellis)." YouTube video. 1:55:09. Apologia Studios. October 9, 2019. https://www.youtube.com/watch?v=vx0rlVap194.

Marsden, George. *Jonathan Edwards, A Life*. New Haven: Yale, 2003.

Marshall, Garry, Joe Glauberg, and Dale McRaven. *Mork and Mindy*. Paramount Television. 1978-1982.

"Newton: The Mechanical Universe." Holisticeducator.com. Accessed July 18, 2022. https://www.holisticeducator.com/newton.htm.

Piper, John. "For Men: Augustine, Sin, and Sovereign Joy." Lecture. The Campus Outreach National Conference: Chattanooga, Tennessee. December 31, 2011.

Piper, John. *The Legacy of Sovereign Joy: God's Triumphant Grace in the Lives of Augustine, Luther, and Calvin.* Vol. 1. Wheaton: Crossway, 2006.

"Plot, The: Ninja Turtle/Mortal Combat Star gets saved." YouTube video. 17:55. Apologia Studios. February 6, 2016. https://www.youtube.com/watch?v=_9WhUtDNSPQ.

Sartelle, John. "Grace-Based Ethics." *Table Talk* online. August 29, 2010. https://www.ligonier.org/learn/devotionals/grace-based-ethics?srsltid=AfmBOooBSNrSlRR2TvzsioBks PxQ_af3j5v0gR-pO50hMMt3wLdfoZlu.

Sproul, R.C. and Stephen J. Nichols, eds. *The Legacy of Luther.* Franklin: Reformation Trust Publishing, 2016.

Sundell, Carl. "The True St. Augustine." *Catholic Insight* online. August 28, 2023. https://catholicinsight.com/the-true-saint-augustine.

Sweeney, Douglas A. *Jonathan Edwards and the Ministry of the Word.* Downer's Grove: InterVarsity Press, 2009.

Tan, Paul Lee. *Encyclopedia of 7,700 Illustrations.* Garland: Bible Communications, Inc., 1996.

Times Square Church. "|Guest| Joni Eareckson Tada | A Deeper Healing." September 24, 2017. YouTube video. 40:44. https://youtu.be/1AP2jeUVt6Y.

About the Author

Jason Murfitt spent a third of his life in the Brazilian rainforest with his wife and firstborn daughter, living among the river-people and an indigenous tribe teaching the Bible. Now with twenty years pastoral experience and two more children, he is presently church-planting on the tiny island of Madeira in the Atlantic. He decided to write *Hope of Glory* to excite Christians who, like himself, want to be braver when speaking about the good news of the gospel, with answers to common objections and thrilling stories to inspire others. His love to help people is insatiable. If you are unable to visit his church in Madeira, then visit his church's website and ask him anything: www.christchurchfunchal.com.

Ambassador International's mission is to magnify the Lord Jesus Christ and promote His Gospel through the written word.

We believe through the publication of Christian literature, Jesus Christ and His Word will be exalted, believers will be strengthened in their walk with Him, and the lost will be directed to Jesus Christ as the only way of salvation.

For more information about
AMBASSADOR INTERNATIONAL
please visit:

www.ambassador-international.com
@AmbassadorIntl
www.facebook.com/AmbassadorIntl

Thank you for reading this book!

You make it possible for us to fulfill our mission, and we are grateful for your partnership.

To help further our mission, please consider leaving us a review on your social media, favorite retailer's website, Goodreads or Bookbub, or our website, and check out some of the books on the following page!

More from Ambassador International

During the time of the Raj in India, Amy Carmichael discovered a custom of the time in which children were 'married to gods' and so introduced to a life of prostitution. With a mixture of courage and heartbreak, she began to uncover the facts, sometimes under disguise, for the government. Against difficult circumstances, Amy and her colleagues provided a safe home for these children against awesomely difficult circumstances at Dohnavur in South India. Until her death in 1951, she devoted fifty years of her life to rescuing babies and children from dangerous backgrounds in India.

George Whitefield made five successful itinerant preaching tours throughout colonial New England, during which he was both appreciated and unwelcomed. Whitefield shook colonial New England, as a blessing to some and as a curse to others. *George Whitefield's Ministry*, written by Kenneth Lawson, is a travelogue of Whitefield's incessant activities to the Puritan and post-Puritan communities.

In *Worldchangers*, challenge your faith as you meet men and women from around the world who turned some of the darkest moments of history into transforming opportunities. Experience the true stories of Christians who lived the adventure of saying yes to a faithful God and be transported to unforgettable moments when ordinary people trusted God for things that seemed impossible and, as a result, changed the world for the better.

www.ingramcontent.com/pod-product-compliance
Lightning Source LLC
Chambersburg PA
CBHW070452100426
42743CB00010B/1585